GW01035079

# Condemned

First published in 2008 by
Liberties Press
Guinness Enterprise Centre | Taylor's Lane | Dublin 8 | Ireland
www.LibertiesPress.com
General and sales enquiries: +353 (1) 415 1224 | peter@libertiespress.com
Editorial: +353 (1) 415 1287 | sean@libertiespress.com

Trade enquiries to CMD Distribution
55A Spruce Avenue | Stillorgan Industrial Park | Blackrock | County Dublin
Tel: +353 (1) 294 2560 | Fax: +353 (1) 294 2564

Distributed in the United States by
Dufour Editions
PO Box 7 | Chester Springs | Pennsylvania | 19425

and in Australia by
James Bennett Pty Limited | InBooks
3 Narabang Way | Belrose NSW 2085

Copyright © Sean Ó Riain, 2008

The author has asserted his moral rights.

ISBN: 978–1–905483–48-8

2 4 6 8 10 9 7 5 3 1

A CIP record for this title is available from the British Library.

Set in Garamond
Cover design by Siné Design
Internal design by Liberties Press
Printed by CPD

This book is sold subject to the condition that it shall not, by way of trade or otherwise, be lent, resold, hired out or otherwise circulated, without the publisher's prior consent, in any form other than that in which it is published and without a similar condition including this condition being imposed on the subsequent publisher.
No part of this publication may be reproduced or transmitted in any form or by any means, electronic or mechanical, including photocopying, recording or storage in any information or retrieval system, without the prior permission of the publisher in writing.

# Condemned

## Letters from Death Row

'Ray' and Seán Ó Riain

To the family of Ray
and
to John M. Ryan and May Hallahan,
parents of Seán Ó Riain

# Contents

# Foreword

The death penalty is the premeditated and cold-blooded killing of a human being by the state. The state can exercise no greater power over a person than that of deliberately depriving him or her of life.

Six decades ago, in December 1948, the UN General Assembly adopted without dissent the Universal Declaration of Human Rights.

The Universal Declaration is a pledge among nations to promote fundamental rights as the foundation of freedom, justice and peace. The rights it proclaims are inherent in every human being. They are not privileges that may be granted by governments for good behaviour and they may not be withdrawn for bad behaviour. Human rights limit what a state may do to any human person.

The Universal Declaration recognises each person's right to life and categorically states further that 'No one shall be subjected to torture or to cruel, inhuman or degrading treatment or punishment'. In Amnesty International's view, the death penalty violates these rights.

There can never be a justification for torture or for cruel, inhuman or degrading treatment or punishment. The cruelty of the death penalty is evident. Like torture, an execution constitutes an extreme physical and mental assault on a person already rendered helpless by government authorities.

If hanging a woman by her arms until she experiences excruciating pain is rightly condemned as torture, how does one describe hanging her by the neck until she is dead? If administering 100 volts of electricity to the most sensitive parts of a man's body evokes disgust, what is the appropriate reaction to the administration of 2,000 volts to his body in order to kill him? If a pistol held to the head or a chemical substance injected to cause protracted suffering are clearly instruments of torture, how should they be identified when used to kill by shooting or lethal injection?

The physical pain caused by the action of killing a human being cannot be quantified. Nor can the psychological suffering caused by foreknowledge of death by execution. Whether a death sentence is carried out six minutes, six weeks or sixteen years after some legal process, the person executed is subjected to uniquely cruel, inhuman and degrading treatment and punishment.

Like killings that take place outside the law, the death penalty denies the value of human life. Many governments have recognised that the death penalty cannot be reconciled with respect for human rights. The UN has declared itself in favour of its abolition. Two-thirds of the world's countries have now abolished the death penalty in law or practice.

The most common justification offered for the death penalty is that, terrible as it is, the death penalty is necessary; it is argued that only the death penalty can meet a particular need of society.

In some countries, the penalty is considered legitimate as a means of preventing or punishing the crime of murder. Elsewhere, it may be deemed necessary to stop drug-trafficking, acts of political terror, economic corruption or adultery. In yet other countries, it is used to eliminate those seen as posing a political threat to the authorities.

Whatever purpose is cited, the idea that a government can justify a punishment as cruel as death conflicts with the very concept of human rights. The significance of human rights is precisely that some means may never be used to protect society because their use violates the very values that make society worth protecting.

Countless men and women have been executed for the stated purpose of preventing crime, especially the crime of murder. Yet Amnesty International has failed to find convincing evidence that the death penalty has any unique capacity to deter others from committing particular crimes.

Undeniably the death penalty, by permanently 'incapacitating' a prisoner, prevents that person from repeating the crime. But there is no way to be sure that the prisoner would indeed have repeated the crime if allowed to live, nor is there any need to violate the prisoner's right to life for the purpose of incapacitation: dangerous offenders can be kept safely away from the public without resorting to execution.

Nor is there evidence that the threat of the death penalty will prevent politically motivated crimes or acts of terror. If anything, the possibility of political martyrdom through execution may encourage people to commit such crimes.

Every society seeks protection from crimes. Far from being a solution, the death penalty gives the false impression that 'firm measures' are being taken against crime. It diverts attention from the more complex measures which are really needed.

When the arguments of deterrence and incapacitation fall away, one is left with a more deep-seated justification for the death penalty: that of just retribution for the particular crime committed. According to this argument, certain people deserve to be killed as repayment for the evil done; there are crimes so offensive that killing the offender is the only just response.

It is an emotionally powerful argument. It is also one which, if valid, would invalidate the basis for human rights. If a person who commits a terrible act can 'deserve' the cruelty of death, why cannot others, for similar reasons, 'deserve' to be tortured or imprisoned without trial, or simply shot on sight? Central to the premise of human rights is that they are inalienable. They may not be taken away even if a person has committed the most atrocious of crimes. Human rights apply to the worst of us as well as to the best of us, which is why they protect all of us.

What the argument for retribution boils down to, is often no more than a desire for vengeance masked as justice. The desire for vengeance can be understood and acknowledged but the exercise of vengeance must be resisted. Vengeance is not, and can never be, justice.

If the law does not sanction the burning of an arsonist's home, the rape of a rapist or the torture of a torturer, it is not because societies tolerate the crimes. Instead, it is because societies understand that they must be built on a different set of values from those which they condemn.

In Ray's case, the family of his victim decided not to pursue the death penalty. In *Condemned*, Seán Ó Riain not only challenges us to see past such empty notions as vengeance as a justification for the death penalty, he also demands that we allow Ray to become fully human, more than the crime he committed or the judgement passed upon him by a court of law.

An execution cannot be used to condemn killing; it *is* killing. Such an act by the state is the mirror image of the criminal's willingness to use physical violence against a victim.

It is the irrevocable nature of the death penalty, the fact that the prisoner is eliminated forever, that makes the penalty so tempting to some states as a tool of repression. Thousands have been put to death under one government only to be recognised as innocent victims when another government comes to power.

When used to crush political dissent, the death penalty is abhorrent. When invoked as a way to protect society from crime, it is illusory. Wherever it is used, it brutalises those involved in the process and conveys to the public a sense that killing a defenceless prisoner is somehow acceptable. It may be used to try to bolster the authority of the state – or of those who govern in its name. But any such authority it confers is spurious. The death penalty is a symbol of terror and, to that extent, a confession of weakness. It is always a violation of the most fundamental human rights.

COLM O'GORMAN, EXECUTIVE DIRECTOR
AMNESTY INTERNATIONAL IRISH SECTION

# Prologue

This book – a mere drop in the ocean of hundreds of books and articles written about the death penalty – is neither a comprehensive description nor an analysis of the death-penalty process. Be that as it may, I cannot think of any redeeming feature in this process. Therefore, *Condemned* unashamedly argues against the death penalty, it tries to raise awareness of the death penalty and it tries to show that this ultimate retribution is biased, racist, cruel and repulsive. That said, nothing in this book is intended to show any disrespect whatsoever to victims of crime.

If people had a fuller understanding of how the death penalty works in the United States of America, they might reject this form of punishment. That is my hope. Human rights are universal, and the abolition of the death penalty should be a matter of concern to the citizens of every country, not just the citizens of the United States. That is my belief.

Most of all I want this book to be a gentle and peaceful narrative of friendship, the friendship between a death-row prisoner and a free-world citizen – between Ray and myself. If I achieve that, I will be very happy. The edited extracts given here are from the letters that we wrote to each other, letters that were not written with publication in mind. They are the letters of two friends which we have decided to share with you, the reader.

I want to humanise my friend, Ray, in the eyes of whoever reads this book. He is a good man who did a bad deed. But each of us is far better than the worst deed we ever committed.

# A Guide for the Reader

The part of the text in *italic* type consists of extracts from the letters of Ray (not his real name) – a prisoner on death row in one of the thirty-six states of the USA which still have capital punishment – to his penfriend in Ireland.

The part of the text in Roman type is written by Ray's penfriend, Seán Ó Riain, and includes extracts from letters he wrote to Ray.

The text in Arial type introduces comments on death row and on the death penalty itself.

# 1

## Ray

The prospect frightened me even though I had been thinking about it for a long time. I feared going into a completely strange situation. Had I the necessary qualities to deal with this situation? Where would it lead me? What if I couldn't communicate? What if I couldn't fulfil the somewhat daunting commitment, which I knew would have to be a lifelong one? From what I had read about the death penalty, I was aware that death-row prisoners are lonely, isolated, rejected people. Perhaps I was drawn to make a commitment to one of these prisoners because of the fact that previously I had worked with homeless people and with the Travelling People, two rejected groups who had brought me happiness and a sense of fulfilment. So after some thought I was satisfied that I was making the right decision and, with the approval and consent of my family, I sought a penfriend among death-row prisoners in the United States of America.

I e-mailed the Rome-based Communita di Sant'Egidio (*www.santegidio.org*): they would send me the name of my new penfriend. I waited for a number of weeks. No word from Rome. This was definitely a positive sign: I was not meant to have a penfriend. But one autumn morning the name did arrive – e-mails arrive so quietly – the name and address of a man in his twenties. This was it. A name and a page of advice, including this: 'To correspond with your penfriend is to know how his feelings are close to ours and to explain this to the other people around us. Of course, our lives are very different but the need to have a friend is the same and this is stronger than any difference that exists.'

So I wrote my first letter to Ray, who is on death row in one of the thirty-six states in the US that still have the death penalty. What would he think of it? What would he think of me? What would he be like?

Dear Ray, I hope it is OK to write to you . . . I enclose a photo so that you can see what I look like! If you try to guess my age and say 'sixty-five, almost sixty-six', you will be correct!

I used to be a teacher but I retired about seven years ago. My wife, Bríd, was a teacher also and we have four children – Francis (37), Catherine (36), Tomás (34) and Liam (28).

Do you know much about Ireland, where I live? I have lived in Dublin since 1964 but I was born in Cork. I had two uncles who went to the US looking for work about 1926. One did well and always had a good job but the other one did not do so well at all. Most Irish people have relations in the US. Thousands left Ireland to go to America looking for work. They started to leave Ireland during and after the Great Famine around 1845, and we have been going to the US ever since. The emigrants used to send money back to their families in Ireland.

Our eldest son, Francis, married a girl from the US but they are living in Ireland now. We went to Chicago for their wedding and also when their two children were born, and we also had a visit to San Francisco . . . We really enjoyed those visits and found the AMerican people very friendly. America is so huge, Ireland is very tiny compared to it, just four million people here altogether.

If it is OK with you, I will write every couple of weeks as a penfriend. I would love to hear from you too – if and when you can. I will not be curious or ask you anything about why you are in prison – that is up to you. I hope you will tell me how you are and how you are coping with prison.

The big prison in Ireland is Mountjoy Prison in Dublin – Bríd and myself go to the stage performance, a drama or a musical, which the prisoners put on every year, and afterwards we get to meet some of the prisoners . . . so we have some very small idea of how prisoners cope with the lack of freedom. We will think of you often and hope that you are well.

Please excuse the typing – it is more mannerly to write by hand but I'm afraid that my handwriting is getting a little wobbly!

Then I waited for three weeks. No reply from the US. This was my chance to escape, but instead I wrote again. Here are a few sentences from my second letter:

Dear Ray, I hope you received my first letter and I hope it was OK . . . It's very easy for me on the outside to write a letter – I just hope that I do not say anything that hurts you . . . If I do, you just tell me!

This year we had the hottest summer for over ten years but now it is getting grey and cold – that is the way it often is in an Irish autumn. We have no extremes of weather in Ireland – we could not even imagine hurricanes like the New Orleans hurricanes. All the deaths and damage were very frightening. Somebody I know in Chicago was at a fund-raising concert to help musicians in New Orleans. In Ireland when we think of New Orleans we think of jazz music.

If you like, tell me about your family. Can they visit you often or are they living far away? As I write it is Friday – tomorrow we will babysit our grandson, Cathal, while his parents visit friends. Cathal is only four months old. He is so small I am nearly afraid to hold him. He is just beginning to smile, so that is very nice.

I will write again soon and in the meantime we will be thinking of you and hoping you are well and coping OK with everything you have to deal with . . . we send you all our best wishes.

I remember clearly that this time I put my name and address on the back of the envelope. I don't know why – it wasn't a habit of mine – but it made all the difference. My letter reached its destination and when a reply came from Ray I knew I had made a commitment that I could never escape from. I'm not sure if that made me happy or not. It certainly frightened me. I remembered other words from Communita di Sant'Egidio: 'This is the most important thing! Don't let your penfriend down. Therefore, please take this into consideration seriously before you start corresponding. At the same time, be careful not to create any expectations you cannot live up to.'

*I must say I was certainly pleased to have gotten this second letter from you. Your first letter was rejected because you didn't put a return address or name on the outside of the envelope. I've actually enclosed the rejection slip. I would've had the letter sent back but I did not have the extra postage at the time. An average letter is 80c to send, which is what they was asking to send this letter you wrote back to you.*

*I enjoyed reading your letter just as I hope you'll enjoy reading mine. Thanks for writing again. Your first letter – could you give that a retake, could I get another introduction letter?!*

*I understood what you meant about being annoying and about informing you of your actions concerning my emotions if you say something offensive or not. Yes, that's understood and I'll be sure to do that. Now this don't just apply to me. You all must also inform me of my actions. In other words, if it appears as if I'm insulting you or anything, before jumping to a conclusion off of an assumption, do you feel what I'm saying? And I'll follow the same advice when it comes from my end of misunderstanding, okay? That way there will always be a mutual understanding when it comes to misunderstandings!*

*I have two sisters, two nieces, a nephew. My mother and father is divorced. I have an eight year old daughter, Rachel, who I love dearly. Yes, they visit, every chance my mother gets to visit or take time off work or have the $ it takes to visit. I'm allowed a visit one day every week. My family try to come down every three or four months. I love getting visits, playing with the kids, kissing my daughter, holding her hands, talking to her. Visiting with loved ones is a wonderful thing here . . . I do a lot of sports to keep my mind off things. I enjoy reading and writing and getting to know people through another's eyes.*

*You say you had one of the hottest summers in ten years. Yes, it was a hot one in the US too. What happened in New Orleans was horrible and then I think along with most Americans, the government job wasn't carried out. The President of the United States, George W. Bush! What do they think of him in Ireland? I'll be shocked if these thoughts are positive! Feel free to speak your mind on that subject! I've visited New Orleans once, it is a city that never leaves one without a place to go or enjoy yourself, if you're of legal age. I think it's a place loved by so many tourists that it'll be restored, maybe better than it was before. What do you think, do you think they'll be able to restore it?*

*I'm glad you didn't let that thought of me not wanting a grey-haired penfriend stop you from writing! Actually I myself have some grey hairs, all on my chin. Grey hairs means wisdom and knowledge is what I was told growing up as a child. I got a question for you. Why did you want to write to me, why me exactly? Just anxious to know, it's not a big deal . . . Well, I'm going to end this now, I didn't say all I could've or wanted to but I must leave something for you to inquire about in your next letter!*

Some weeks later I received this letter from Paul, an inmate in the general population in the same prison as Ray.

'Hello! How are you? Fine, I hope. . . . It's strange how I stumbled upon your information. My job at the moment is trash detail and I found your letter with photo and postcard enclosed. Needing someone to correspond with, I decided to write. I hope you don't mind. I see that you wrote to another person housed at this facility so if there is a problem with me writing to you, from either you or Ray, I apologize and will cease to write immediately. . . . As you can see my name is Paul. I am a 6 foot, 220lb, black male. . . . From your postcard, Dublin looks beautiful. I would love to visit when I am free from prison. Speaking of which, I'm looking forward to being released from here sometime this year. I've been incarcerated for eleven years and I am thirty-two years of age as of yesterday. . . . Prison has been very educational. If one apply himself, there's many things to learn, both positive and negative. But most of all, it enables one to learn of self! . . . I spend my days reading, going to school for crafts, sometimes basketball and nearly all the time Scrabble. I also play chess. But chess requires a lot of patience, which I don't have. . . . I see you were in education. What did you teach? And at what grade level? What did your wife teach? I'm not a very educated person, yet I've always found Math to be mystical, so my interest enabled me to understand it thoroughly. . . . I'm interested in learning of different cultures and countries. I've heard that it's easy living in Ireland. Did I hear wrong? . . . I would really like to keep a line of communication with you. If you don't find this to be possible, no problem. Take care and hope to hear from you soon, Paul.'

It was annoying that a prison authority could, with almost no justification, just throw my personal letter on the garbage heap. It showed little respect for me or for the person to whom the letter was addressed. I did not reply to Paul. Sometimes that bothers me. Was I guilty of what I condemned in others – lack of respect? I did not hear from Paul again.

* * *

*I received your letter and the photos, thanks, it's always nice to have a face to go with the words. I'll send you a photo of me when I'm able to take one again. I truly think we'll get on fine. I will share with you as time goes on and trust is built.*

*Yes, Rosa Parks did pass a while ago. What she did was part of history and they spoke of it a lot in school, how things used to be back when the color of one's skin was frowned upon.*

*I don't know much of anything about Ireland so I look forward to future conversations about your homeland. I liked the legend you sent me about Lake Derravaragh and the Children of Lir. I would like to visit Ireland some day. One of my favorite actors is from Ireland. Colin Farrell. Are you familiar with him? You've been over to the States a few times and you thought the people were friendly and you enjoyed your stay here. That's nice.*

*You're concerned with how I cope in this place – well, I must say some days are tougher than others but it must be dealt with for I have a loving mother, sisters, Rachel – my lovely daughter I haven't spent any time with beyond these walls, nieces and nephew, all of which was born after my incarceration. I'm motivated by them. I also cope because I feel I'll return to freedom. I have a lot of issues in my case that should work in my favor, I have faith in the good Lord and I want to prove to the nay-sayer that I can be a productive citizen out in the world, I've grown a lot since I came here and I'd like to make the ones I've disappointed throughout my lifetime proud of what I've become now. I think it's very good that there's people out in the world who's willing to extend a hand to those who's made mistakes in their life.*

*So me and your youngest son is about the same age. You said you and your family went to the dramas in Mountjoy, now that's a thought-provoking name for a prison. I'm sure it's not that joyous there, wonder have any of the prisoners ever tried to sue for false advertising! We don't do such things as have stage performances like you spoke of, no way, nothing even close. We used to have talent shows amongst the inmates here, poetry readings, singing, drawing, things of that nature. They don't have talent shows anymore. They stopped letting us have them because the inmates started getting boastful and nit-picky, provoking the others who didn't win, and it caused fights and hate, so they stopped it all. Isn't that disgraceful? I have a lot of poetry I've written over the years. Here are a few lines:*

*Sirens echoing through the streets*
*Late at night, so it's hard to sleep.*
*So instead I stare out of my bedroom*
*Window, and it's drug dealers*
*And users I see.*
*Amazed by their swagger as I gazed from afar,*
*I made a wish that night –*
*I wished to be 'just like they are'.*

*And out of all my childhood wishes that was the one that had to come true. . . . I consider my poetry to be profane and dark. I write a lot, it helps me channel my emotions and it helps relieve stress. And now, my new-found friend, I'm going to end this letter. Until next time take care of yourself. Thanks for writing and tell your lovely wife I said hi. I enjoyed writing this. By the way, I don't know if you know this or not but I'm not just in prison. I've been sentenced to death, I'm on death row. Did you know this or just thought I was in prison?*

And so that autumn Ray and I started to exchange letters, one every fortnight or so. Sometimes the letters crossed in the post and then questions had to wait to be answered. Communita di Sant'Egidio had advised not to 'ask for the reason why somebody has been condemned to death. If he wants to tell you, he will do so. It is, however, extremely important to check with your penfriend that he is not giving up his rights out of despair, by dismissing his lawyer or asking to be voluntarily put on the execution list.' I already felt that there was no chance at all that Ray would take one of those extreme steps.

I did not ask him why he was on death row, I already knew. Despite my earlier protestations that I would not be curious, I had looked up his case on the internet, where there seems to be no privacy. I knew Ray's age, his height and his place of birth, I knew he was on death row for one of the most common crimes – a killing during a robbery. I told Ray that I knew from the start that he was on death row and that I also knew all those other things about him. That was fine and we just began to relax with each other, albeit at a distance of thousands of miles across the ocean. I looked forward to the regular letters, the address in Ray's copperplate handwriting, the prison logo prominent on the envelope, along with the franked statement giving the origin of the letter. I have never got used to the chilling fact that these letters come from the death row of a US prison.

# 2

# Why?

Why, then, was I writing to a death-row prisoner – and a guilty one at that? I think the seeds were sown early. My parents were always sympathetic to anybody who was down on his luck. My mother never went into the city without making sure she had coins in her pocket 'in case I meet a poor person'.

I still remember clearly, and often think about, two people whom I met just briefly when I was in my teens. At the back of our house there were miles and miles of unspoiled countryside, a river, small bog lakes, fish, birds, foxes and otters. It was a paradise. A railway line ran from the city along the edges of the fields and out to west Cork. One day we met a young boy who had escaped from a well-known reformatory school and was making his way into the city along the railway line, avoiding the road. He was heading for Dublin, 150 miles away. He was very cold in his thin shirt. We had no money to help him. Another day a few years later, at the end of my teens, when I was a member of the Franciscans, I remember walking with two or three fellow friars along a narrow country lane in the west of Ireland when the morning frost was still hard on the fields. We came to a Traveller camp. In the corner of the camp was a tent, its canvas damp, cold and frozen stiff with the frost. Inside, a youth lay shivering under a thin blanket. We had a vow of poverty. We had no money to help him. I have often wondered what became of that youth. He could have been Tom, a Traveller I knew, who on a cold winter's night in 1985 died from exposure in rich south county Dublin, a couple of miles from where I live.

I have always thought that prisons are the most horrible places on earth. Also, in my heart I feel that the death penalty is repulsive, and the ultimate horror to me is keeping a man on death row for ten, twenty or more years before the system kills him, coldly, clinically. That man's death certificate says 'legal homicide'. I have always felt sorry for people who advocate and support this death-row system, the people who say 'an eye for an eye, a life for a life'. One reason I feel sorry for them is that they can never, I believe, pray the most beautiful prayer of all, the 'Pater Noster': forgive us our trespasses as we forgive those who trespass against us.

All my experiences and reading over forty years have shown me that it is a good thing to write in unquestioning friendship to a prisoner on death row. In her book *Stolen Time*, Sunny Jacobs, who was herself wrongly condemned to death until she was finally exonerated in 1992, wrote: 'We in prison depend on those we have left outside for our very existence. Without their support and acknowledgement we cease to exist in the outside world.' Writing to a death-row prisoner needs no further justification than those words.

I remember too the man in the west Kerry Gaeltacht who, as we worked at the hay, said '*Níl teora leis an trócaire*' – 'There is no limit to compassion'. Again, total justification.

I was involved for over twenty years in caring and campaigning groups for the homeless and for the Travelling People. Then, as I grew older, I thought that writing to a death-row prisoner might be less strenuous than working with homeless people or with Travellers. It *was* less strenuous, but it wasn't any easier. People say: 'You're good, that kind of thing is easy for you.' Wrong on both counts: it is not easy for anybody, and I write to Ray not because I'm good but because I'm trying to be good.

# 3

## The Letters and More . . .

Dear Ray . . . You asked about George W. Bush! We've been on the anti-war marches in Dublin, one march had 150,000 people at it. There is a very strong anti-war feeling in Ireland and it's hard not to say 'we told you so' when we see the terrible suffering of Iraqis and of US soldiers. US warplanes land at Shannon Airport in Ireland to re-fuel on the way to and from Iraq. That is causing a lot of controversy – it brings a certain amount of revenue, so some people are for it, but many others suspect that some of the planes carry prisoners who are being brought to countries where they can be tortured. At the moment there is a trial in Dublin of five young people – one of them, a girl, is a US citizen – who damaged a US warplane in Shannon Airport so that it could not fly. They admit the action but are claiming that they were justified because disabling the plane meant that lives in Iraq were saved. The verdict is due any day. . . . I think one of the worst things is that when you criticise some aspect of US policy, people say you are anti-American. I hate the war in Iraq but I am not anti-US: I had a cousin and an uncle in the US army.

Regarding writing: Marsha Hunt, a black woman who used to be a girlfriend of Mick Jagger, the singer – before your time! – lived for a while in Dublin, where she organised a writing course for prisoners in Mountjoy Jail. The prisoners' writings were published. It may be out of print, but if it's still in print I will try to get the publishers to send you a copy. Still on writing – I enclose three short pieces I wrote, one about Dorothy Day; the second piece mentions Travellers, who are a nomadic people in Ireland, only about two thousand families altogether, not very popular but I like them; the third piece is about our back garden. I hope you like them and that they don't upset you because they are full of nostalgia – wait for a good day to read them! Criticism welcome.

Let us know how many $ we should send you. Don't be shy to say. Finally, a word of Irish/Gaelic for you! *Slán* (pronounced 'slawn') is what you say when you are leaving a person. It means 'goodbye' but it also means 'fare well, be well'. So until we speak again, *slán*, goodbye.

*Thanks for the postcards – I found the statue of James Larkin more interesting than the postcard of the Dublin Spire because there's a story to go along with his life.*

*You said in your letter that I sounded strong but thanks for saying that if I'm not feeling so preppy I could hold off on writing. Well, I'm usually for the most part holding up well. Holidays and certain family-gathering-thought-provoking days get me down, Xmas, birthdays, Thanksgiving, but over the years one learns how to cope better. When I first got here it was very hard to cope, not only with that, but to be facing such a sentence as death and knowing there's people out there in the world that would rather see you dead than living, and these people don't even know anything about you. That gets to me at times when I just sit around and dwell on it but I try to keep my mind occupied with different things – reading, writing, basketball, watching TV, listening to the radio or just talking to the other inmates here about current events, sports, music or women. We usually start up a conversation that causes one another to laugh or think of other things besides the situation we're faced with. Writing to you like this helps a lot to escape this place and the reality of my situation. As you'll see as the time goes by and you get to know me, I very rarely speak about this place and what goes on here. Why, you may be wondering? Well, I have to be here 24 hours a day, 7 days a week, 365 days a year, so I like to escape by talking about your life and the things going on outside of this place. Do that make sense?*

*But since you asked about prison life! We eat breakfast at 4 AM except on Sunday morning when we eat at 6 AM, lunch at 11 AM, dinner at 3 PM, the trays are brought to the cell and that's the food for the day unless you have some canteen-bought food. There isn't much you can get for free. You would think with charging us for everything from food to toiletries to medication to writing material we would be allowed work to earn $ but no, so we must depend on family and friends. We buy our 13" TVs if we can afford them. We shower every other day. We're allowed out of the cell – 8' x 5' – once every day for one hour which is usually when we go outside to shoot basketball, lift weights or just walk around the walk yard and talk to the other inmates and friends.*

*I can call home – all our calls are collect calls – every second week and talk to my mother and Rachel when I can catch her in the house! I also have a few friends I can call. We can't call out of the country.*

*As for the administration at the prison, there are some good and some rotten ones. They do random cell searches every night and they do major searches about twice a year and it's not pretty, it's like they just have to throw your things all over the place. The worst part is having to put everything back in order. You asked do we have educational courses. Not anymore, they used to have courses but it was stopped for some reason so now there's no educational courses.*

*The worst days of all is when there's an execution scheduled, and even worse when it's someone close to you or someone you've a bond with. Since I've been here there's been about a dozen executions. I was close with three of them, I mean I associated with them, and was deeply saddened to see them go. . . .*

Work on death row also takes its toll on prison officers. In December 2007, two former South Carolina prison officers filed a lawsuit against the South Carolina Department of Corrections (SCDC) alleging that they were forced to participate in executions, including botched lethal-injection and electrocution executions.

Major Craig Baxley was in charge of the SCDC's SWAT team, used in emergencies in institutions throughout the state. Baxley claims that SCDC had made it clear that he could not acquire and hold the team-leader position unless he agreed to act as an executioner of condemned inmates, a position which was outwardly represented as 'voluntary'. During the course of his service, Baxley said that he killed eight inmates and participated in two other executions. Although these executions were barbaric, gruesome and repulsive to Major Baxley, he continued to perform them in order to be able to continue as team leader and to draw the financial benefits of his position as a major. Baxley also claims that the SCDC made two others act as executioners when it was clear that neither wanted to do so voluntarily. It is claimed that one eventually committed suicide and the other was forced into disability retirement.

*I don't mingle with a lot of the inmates, I have my collected group of friends and just speak and keep it moving with the rest. It's not wise to have too many friends here, it sometimes can turn out bad, you know? I've been in a few fights since I came here, all of them results of the basketball court, but that was during my early stay here, when I was younger and my temper was short. I've grown over the years and don't let a lot of things bother me as I did when I was younger.*

*Yes, it is very good that I can see my daughter and the rest of my loved ones. I wish I could see them more but I must work with the working schedule of my mother and when she can come. As long as breath is in my body, I'll forever love my mother, sisters and father and all of the kids, and I pray they'll always love me the same way. As the priest at your sister-in-law's renewal of wedding vows said: 'There is only one response when somebody says they love you – Yipee!'*

*As I write I'm counting my blessings to have you and your wife come into my life. The group that gave you my name, I've heard of it before, yes, I think they're a good and practical group. I've only heard good things about them, I know they found many inmates friends to write to them. I've never wrote to them and asked them to find me someone to write to, so I don't know how they came up with my name.*

*You are lucky as you all are still able to baby-sit and spend time with your grandkids. I hope and pray I'm still be around to meet and hold my grandkid or kids. Lord willing, I'll be here on earth and out in the world to help Rachel raise them up to be productive citizens. I wrote these lines for her:*

> *From the window of my prison cell, I gaze at a star so bright that fills the sky, I think about my baby girl – you!*
>
> *From the window of my prison cell as I look out into the dark but bright sky, I silently begin to cry.*
>
> *Every tear is cried for you as I wish I was there to hold you and gaze upon your face as I gaze on this star at night.*
>
> *If I could hold you, I bet my face would light up, just as bright as the daytime sky itself.*
>
> *And even though I can't hold you at this time,*
>
> *I've just named the star after you, the star that's always in my sights, in front of my prison cell window, the star that shines so bright throughout the night.*

*I will send you some of the more profane poetry one of these days but not right now! No, my friend, it's not a shocker to me how you feel about George Bush! I personally feel the same way just like a lot of other people I know. As in Ireland, there has been anti-war protests here – there's the mother of a fallen soldier protesting in front of the President's ranch house in Texas. She requested a sit-down talk with the President but he wouldn't meet with her so then she organised the protest and then they put her in jail.*

*Isn't that something? Tell me, what was the outcome to the trial for the five young'uns who damaged the US plane in Shannon? I imagine your legal system isn't as harsh as it is over here in the US, is it?*

*The book of writings by prisoners in Mountjoy that Marsha Hunt put together sounds an interesting read, I would like to read it if possible. I do know who Mick Jagger is! 'Satisfaction', I liked that song and another one I liked from the Rolling Stones, 'You Can't Always Get What You Want'.*

*If you're willing to do so, you can send a money order to Michael, he's my closest friend, I call him my uncle. He was once a penfriend to me but over the years he's become part of my family. If you send it to him, make it out to him, he'll cash it and buy another one that's allowed by the prison, he knows how to handle the process. I've already spoken of you and your wife to him and that you was from Ireland. I've known Michael for about eight years. He's been a loyal and faithful friend to me since the beginning and he has love for me and me for him just like he's my uncle. As for how much you should send, would $50 be too much? Honestly, whatever you're able to send would be appreciated and put to good use, so it's really up to you.*

*This is a very long letter, isn't it? I enjoyed writing it and I hope you enjoy reading it and I didn't bore you to sleep with all I spoke about. But you asked about the prison and I gave you all that came to mind as I wrote! If there's anything more you'd like to know, feel free to ask, okay? Again take care and thanks for listening – or reading in our case!*

I sent some dollars to Michael. As I got to know Ray, at the same time I developed great admiration for Michael as we exchanged occasional e-mails. He told me a little about his distant Irish roots, we had in common our opposition to the invasion of Iraq, we agreed on other social issues. He was gentle and kind. He told me nothing of his long and devoted commitment to Ray – that I discovered from Ray himself. He replied: 'I wanted you to know that the money arrived and has been forwarded. Please don't misunderstand when I mention that you should make a careful decision about Ray because he does seem to become dependent upon those on the outside, and he has been severely disappointed many times. People quit writing or sharing. He has no other source of income, and his family members are very poor. I never ask him what he does with the money, so I cannot tell you whether he is careful or careless about it. I feel that a gift is a gift, and that is the end of it. I certainly don't mind being your conduit since he is only allowed a few names to include on his lists. His circumstances sound dreadful, but as he has said many times: "We have to work with them", meaning the prison officials. Yes, he is a delightful young man in many ways. I can't help but wonder what his life might have been like under different circumstances. You will continue to enjoy his insights.'

The death penalty is a poor person's issue. Supreme Court Justice Sandra Day O'Connor said that poor people are at greater risk of being wrongly put to death because of the defence they are likely to receive. Referring to a study in Texas, Judge O'Connor said that people charged with murder with court-appointed attorneys were 28 percent more likely to be convicted and 44 percent more likely to be sentenced to death if convicted than people who had enough money to hire an attorney. Poor people don't get to choose their attorneys. In Alabama more than half of the state's death-row prisoners are represented by court-appointed attorneys who, under state law, could only spend $1,000 preparing for trial. A comprehensive two-year study scrutinised the role of race, economic status and other factors in about 1,500 homicide cases in Nebraska since 1973 and found that criminals were more than three times as likely to receive the death penalty if they had murdered someone relatively rich.

The anti-death penalty campaigner Sister Helen Prejean claims that when 'nobodies' are killed, law-enforcement officers seem hardly to notice, much less vigorously prosecute the perpetrator. One study of forty families of mainly African-American murder victims showed that not only had none of them seen the murderers charged with a capital crime, not one had seen a case brought to trial. In some cases, there had not even been an investigation of the murder.

In January 2007, there were 3,350 people on death row in the United States. Ten years earlier, in a letter to Pope John Paul II, Sr Prejean said that 99 percent of the 3,100 people then on death row were poor. She further wrote: 'I have found that as a general rule those involved in justice for poor people readily oppose the death penalty whereas those separated from poor people and their struggles readily support it. They are more prone to see poor people as the "enemy" and to be willing to inflict harsh punishment to "control" them.'

I can understand those words when I think of my own experiences with the Travelling People. If, for one reason or another, I have not met any Travellers for a couple of weeks, then I notice that it becomes easier to nod one's head in agreement with anti-Traveller sentiment in the mass media. When I find this happening to me, I know it is time to get out and about again, it is time to meet Travellers, time to hear their story from themselves.

# 4

## Sharing Our Writing Styles

*I got your letter a few days ago and it found me doing fine. I was saddened by the news of the car accident. My friend, you got to be more careful out there, how am I to further our friendship if you're not able to correspond and share with me the things occupying your mind, ya know?! Until the next time, take care of yourself, stay out of accidents and tell your wife I said hi. Thanks for spending the time it takes to write to me, it's very appreciated.*

*I'd never heard of Dorothy Day until you told me about her, so I was enlightened about what she stood for. It's evident that she wanted to do more than just exist on earth. Is your writing a job or something you just find joy in doing?*

*You stated I could give criticism! Well, the piece concerning the priest and the Travellers – I didn't really get it, it was all over the place. I didn't know if it was a part of your actual writing to me or what, so I must say it confused me more than anything. So I will ask, was you sharing with me your own experiences about life in the monastery, or was it the priest speaking? And a lot of the words I couldn't identify with like 'nomadic people', who are those? There was a lot of words I was thrown with like Franciscan and some others. I couldn't help but feel like you forgot to translate some of the story, you wrote it without taking into consideration that all of this is new to me. I only have an 8th grade education and after reading this second piece, it really made me feel like it!*

*Now my favorite is the third piece which I enjoyed dearly and certainly understood and enjoyed the message. I would like to know how the sport of hurling is played, it sounds sort of like what we over here call baseball, do you know of it? And yes, I understood what you meant about giving anything to be able to start afresh. I feel the same way about my life.*

Ray is an honest if strict critic, so I'll only give the third piece, the one he liked and enjoyed! The piece was called *The Pyracantha Bush.*

> It's years since the man in the garden centre said that pyracantha would be ideal for the back wall – four bushes, two with red berries, two with orange berries, they would grow tall and prickly and colourful.
>
> So we did what the man suggested and, of course, he was right. The four bushes are a mass of white flowers in May, and by October they are brilliant with red and orange colour. When the weather hardens, the blackbirds feast, and when the winter is really bad, field fares and redwings come down from the Dublin Mountains – how do they find out about our red and orange berries? One year we had a glorious flock of bramblings, every year we have redpolls and a pair of goldfinches and sometimes we have a menacing sparrow hawk.
>
> Just when the pyracantha bushes had grown and spread their branches wide enough to cover the concrete of the back wall, our children discovered the joys of hurling in the local club. I should never have told them the story of how Christy Ring brought his hurley with him and practised everywhere he went, because soon they were all practising their aim and sharpening their eye against the back wall. *Wham* went the sliotar. 'Yah, good shot.' *Thud* went the sliotar. 'Ah, keep it low . . . No, whoever puts the ball over the wall goes around to get it.' *Wham.*

And soon the constant practice, the puck of the ball against the wall, the honing of skills, improving that all-important first touch, settling the nerves before gathering the gear bag and heading off to the match, trying to look nonchalant – it all took its toll on the two bushes in the centre. With unerring aim, the sliotar picked off the lower branches one by one and soon a big arc of the concrete wall was revealed – every bit as ugly and bare as it was the day we first planted the pyracantha bushes.

But then as the 'children' left one after the other, the branches reached out and covered the concrete wall once more . . . I remember the poem of Séamus Ó Néill who curbed the urge that rose in him to wipe the marks of jam from the door. He reminded himself that the day would soon come when the door would be clean and the small hands that had left their sticky imprint would be gone. . . .

*Bhí subh milis*
*ar bhaschrann an dorais,*
*ach mhúch mé an corraí*
*ionam a d'éirigh,*
*mar smaoinigh mé ar an lá*
*a bhéas an baschrann glan,*
*agus an lámh bheag*
*ar iarraidh.*

And so it is now with us . . . But I'd give anything to be starting out afresh and to have the wall bare and ugly again. . . .

Today dust-covered hurleys stand idle in the side passage and I know that if I looked I'd find a sliotar in that old drawer in the corner. I have seen their faces glowing as they recall childhood memories of good games and thrilling runs down the wing . . . And come All-Ireland day or maybe next summer, if I can gather them all together – even for a short while – we might wipe the dust off the hurleys and give the pyracantha bushes one last fright. And then let them grow as they were meant to.

* * *

I went to buy the Christmas tree a few days ago – on account of my injured ribs from the car accident, I was afraid to do any lifting so I asked a friend, Rahim, to help me. That is not an Irish name! Rahim is an asylum-seeker from Afghanistan. He came here about a year ago with his friend; their lives were in danger. I got to know the two of them earlier this year when I started visiting a centre for asylum-seekers. It's about two miles away – some local people go there every Thursday to be friends to the asylum-seekers. There are people there from Africa – Congo, Nigeria, Rwanda, Somalia, Zimbabwe, Algeria – and also from Iran and different parts of Russia, men, women and children. They are cheerful and brave but also very sad, there have been very sad events in their lives back home. Isn't it amazing how people who are suffering are so brave? On Thursdays we have a lovely time with talk and chat and lots of laughs – it does me a lot of good. So this has been our year for getting to know new people from all over the world – this time last year we didn't think we would know you.

What I started out to say was that the Christmas tree cost €50, I think that's about $60. Everything is very expensive in Ireland, I got a haircut the other day . . . I know you will wonder why I need a haircut at all! It cost €8 and Rahim said that back in Afghanistan you could buy a cow for that amount of money! Rahim is a Muslim, a very nice guy, very peace-loving. They have a very big feast day in Afghanistan every year where the richer people will buy a cow and give a third to relations, keep a third for themselves and give a third to poor people.

Recently about two hundred asylum-seekers from Afghanistan had a demonstration outside Dáil Éireann – that's our parliament – in support of their case to be allowed stay in Ireland. Rahim always rightly complains that asylum-seekers can do nothing – they are not allowed work, for example – and so when his sister phones him, he never has any news for her. Now, I said, you can tell her about the demonstration. 'I can't,' he laughed, 'she would think I was in great danger because in Afghanistan if somebody complains or demonstrates, they simply disappear and are never seen again! So I can't worry her.'

*This is our first Christmas together and I look forward to being part of many more as a family friend. I'll be thinking of you all at Christmas and I hope this upcoming year is filled with joy and blessings for all the family. You two take care and know I'm grateful to have friends like you.*

*I appreciated your Christmas wishes. It was a peaceful Christmas. We got our parcels – we are allowed them for the holidays but we or our friends must pay for them, nothing is free. I'm enclosing a list of the things we are allowed, things we are unable to get throughout the year. Other than that there's nothing special going on, it's just another day as far as the prison is concerned. But I did have a peaceful Christmas. I talked on the phone to my mom, couldn't get in touch with my sisters or daughter – they were gone to a party, my father don't have a phone. When I first got here the first three years was very tough for me around this time of year, wishing to be with family and thinking back on all the memories from growing up. It's gotten a lot easier to bear now but one can't get used to being away from loved ones.*

*You was right about me being glad Christmas is over, not that I have anything against it. It's just with my being away from my loved ones and family, not being able to do the things I was used to doing at this time of year, it's not that easy. With the reminiscing and then all the reminders being shown on TV, the activities going on in the shopping malls, TV shows showing all the traditional things families do at this time, it's hard not to miss family and freedom. And then not only that, during this time of year the prisons take so many holidays off where there isn't mail etc. Yes, I'm surely glad the holidays are over . . . It sounds like you all had a nice time, the family showed up, you ate good, conversed, laughed and collected memories for the future which is always good. Noisy is good, that means it's life being enjoyed and shared.*

*As I said, I didn't get a visit from the family this year. The money was funny and Mom couldn't afford it . . . Yes, it's hard to say all that's needed to be said during a visit. In spite of all the downers within a visit, the higher moments outweigh them all. Just being in the presence of loved ones, seeing them smile. It's always the saddest at 2.25* PM *when it's time to part. That's hard every time, I know it's that way for everyone. I have not to look back once I get my last hugs and kisses. Once I looked back and saw my mother's face, it crushed my whole insides. After I walk through the door and get searched by the guards, I go around to the window of the visiting room where usually my sisters are standing. That's our last 'Take care. I love you' before I leave. I blow air kisses to them. Visits are beautiful things, the splitting up afterwards is the hard part. I always sit with my back to the clock. If not, I'll watch it all the visit.*

*I nearly forgot to mention – I was very pleased and honored to have a Christmas card of mine on your mantelpiece with all the others.*

Shortly after that Christmas the *Irish Independent* reported that 'the State of California has executed a seventy-six-year-old blind and deaf man for organising a triple murder twenty-five years ago to silence witnesses in another killing. Clarence Ray Allen, who was also wheelchair-bound, had to be assisted into the execution chamber by four prison officers before being put to death by lethal injection in the early hours of the morning. He is the second-oldest man to be given the death penalty since the US resumed capital punishment in 1977. Allen was already serving a life sentence for murder when he masterminded the murder of three people who were due to testify against him during his appeals. The US Supreme Court rejected last-minute arguments that he was so old and sick his execution would constitute cruel and unusual punishment.'

*You said you measured out the size of my cell – 8' x 5' – in your kitchen. Yes, it is small. Now add inside that 8' x 5' a six-foot bed attached to one side of the wall and a two-foot desk to write on behind the bed. That's one side of the cell. Then there's the sink and below the sink is the toilet. I'll get you a picture of me inside my cell so you can see what I'm talking about, very small living quarters for sure but one must cope if he wants to survive. I was always told that the strong is the only ones that survive and I personally consider myself one of the strongest on this planet! So I must cope, if not for myself, for those who believe in my coming out of this place.*

*You use to play basketball! So you know how addictive that can be. I love basketball, always have since I was a kid, I used to play for the community center and I was fairly good. My favorite player is Kobe Bryant of the LA Lakers, ever heard of him? Thanks for explaining the game of hurley with your drawing of the goals and how you score. You asked would you make a good artist – well, going by your drawings, I don't think so!!*

*So your daughter, Catherine, and her husband, Martin, are going to Africa, I would love to travel there – the place they are going to visit. I'd never even heard of Senegal but I know there's a lot of needy residents in Africa that need assistance with living. If everyone in the world had more compassion for the less fortunate, there wouldn't be so much hate and violence, wouldn't you agree? I would be honored to see some photos from their trip. I'm sure it will be much different from where they live in County Clare.*

*Oh, I saw Mary Robinson, who was President of Ireland, on TV the other day and I instantly thought of you all over there. Usually I wouldn't look at anything like this, but I watched in honor of my new Irish friends.*

I completely forgot to tell you, Ray, about the trial of the people who damaged the US warplane in Shannon Airport – well, the trial collapsed again. This is the second trial that collapsed, this time because the judge was a guest at G. W. Bush's inauguration – the first one, I think – and was also a guest at something else organised by the president – so when the defence lawyers raised this matter the judge agreed that it could be seen that he might be biased and so declared a no-trial. A new trial has been set for next July – that will make it four years since the offence was committed and the arguments are starting now about whether this is fair or not. The defendants admit they damaged the plane but they are arguing that they had 'just cause'. There are five defendants, three are strong but I've heard that at least one is under serious stress – it has been very hard on them. They are on bail, not in custody.

* * *

*So you attended a monastery to become a priest. You stated it wasn't for you. In what sense, why didn't you like it? If you could today would you go back and give it a shot again? The religion you joined, the Franciscans, I'd never heard of until we started writing to each other. Is it true monks can't indulge in physical pleasure with a lady?*

*What are your beliefs exactly? I was brought up in a Baptist church and was raised as a Christian. However, as I grew older and learned more, I tended not to embrace 'religion'. I think that religion complicates life, regardless of which it is. Life is complicated enough without the guidelines of religions. I do believe in a higher power like God Almighty and having a sense of spirituality is wonderful. But I look at people like those over in the Middle East, who's supposedly killing over religious purposes, and it's not right. If everyone believes in a God,* the *God, why should it matter who the Prophets are? I don't get that. How is one to know what to believe besides there is a power greater than man? I don't know.*

*Thanks for photos, especially the one of you and your grandson, Cathal, – this is a nice picture for sure. I got a good laugh with what you stated on the back of it – 'Two Baldies'. The garden is beautiful – whoever takes care of it is doing a good job. It would be a nice play area for a dog but with a dog there would be no nice garden, I suppose. I liked the rainbow over the garden – it's said that at the end of a rainbow there's a pot of gold and a leprechaun.*

'Indeed it seems to me that the more Christian a country is, the less likely it is to regard the death penalty as immoral. Abolition has taken its firmest hold in post-Christian Europe and has least support in the church-going United States. I attribute that to the fact that for the believing Christian, death is no big deal' – Justice Antonin Scalia of the US Supreme Court, a practising Catholic, in a pro-death penalty paper, 'God's Justice and Ours', delivered at a conference of the Pew Forum on Religion and Public Life in 2002.

Bud Welch is also a practising Catholic. His daughter, Julie, was murdered in the Oklahoma City bombing in April 1995. Six years later, the bomber, Timothy McVeigh, was executed. By then most of the 168 victims' families thought his execution was irrelevant in so far as it did nothing to heal their hurt, which would last to the day they died. Welch said 'I've met Bill McVeigh, Tim's father. He's suffering more than I am. I brag about Julie to everyone I meet but what can Bill McVeigh say about his son? I'd rather be me than him any day.' He spoke of driving once with Julie when the news came through on the car radio of an execution in Texas. Julie remarked that the death penalty was nothing but vengeance, 'it just fuels hate'. Welch said that the killing of Timothy McVeigh dishonoured Julie. 'I'm Catholic, I believe in the sanctity of all life, not just innocent life but the lives of mass murderers also.' Today Bud Welch is a member of Murder Victims' Families for Human Rights.

*I got your letter today and I also got* The Junk Yard, *the book of prisoner writing in Mountjoy. I have read some of it and it is certainly my kind of book. I've always been intrigued by true stories of struggle, listening to others' stories and comparing them.*

*I'd like for you to read* Manchild in the Promised Land *by Claude Brown, if you can find it over there. It's pretty similar to how I came up and the things that was going on around where I was growing up. Heroin wasn't the drug of choice, it was crack cocaine that destroyed everything. When I read that book I saw myself throughout the entire book, it's the autobiography of Brown, when you get a chance check it out for me and let me know what you think.*

*About the $, I do appreciate you sending them. I can buy things I need, soap etc, and even some things I just desire to have. So 'bob' is slang for money over there. Well, over here, we say bread, cake or cheese or flow, which do you prefer?! I mostly say bread or cake.*

*I liked the story about Setanta. It's the same here, it's the older people who tell stories. What's your take on that? About my poems – if I re-write them, it'll take away the rawness. I write with the heart. If I dwelled and dwelled on what I write, then it's like I'm cheating, it's not directly from the heart. My favorite poet is Khalil Gibran. Another of my favorite authors is Maya Angelou and Ralph Waldo Emerson.*

# 5

## Mitigating Circumstances

*You apologize for not writing sooner. Let me state that I understand that you have a life outside of writing to me, so when your time don't allow you to do so, it's nothing you have to apologize for.*

*I went outside yesterday, shot some basketball and one of the guys came down on my back and it's been hurting ever since. I've had this injury before, I just got to chill out and let it heal itself. Right now I just sit on a pillow, try to keep it straight upward, it's my lower back. So writing this letter to you is a lot of work for me, got me sitting here like I'm in military school or something!*

*No, I don't really know what this year brings me. I might hear something concerning my appeal – I went to court to get some important papers from the DA's office, the judge allowed this but the attorney general appealed and the decision was that I didn't need the paperwork. Then my lawyers appealed to the Supreme Court and that's where things are now. I trust my lawyers will get me the result I want which is a new trial because I didn't have an effective lawyer and I think that if I had I wouldn't be sitting here on death row. At my trial I was floored by the guilty verdict for capital murder. I'll tell you why I wasn't supposed to have been found guilty in the future, it's a long story but I promise I'll share it in the future. I know for certain that if I had the proper representation when I was going to trial, I would be back out in the world right now.*

No matter what other death-penalty reforms are undertaken, if defendants on trial do not have a defence team competent enough to challenge the prosecution's evidence, wrong verdicts are inevitable. Judge Ruth Bader Ginsburg, speaking in support of a moratorium on executions and quoted by Sr Helen Prejean in her book *The Death of Innocents,* said that people 'who are well represented at trial do not get the death penalty. I have yet to see a death-penalty case among the dozens coming to the Supreme Court on eve-of-execution stay applications in which the defendant was well-represented at trial.'

*You asked about my childhood. Well, I grew up with two younger sisters. My mother and father were both addicted to crack cocaine and from the age of twelve years old I had to provide for myself and my sisters. And I did that by stealing out of stores for food and clothes or just going to friends of the family who knew our situation, begging for what it was we needed. I did that until I was fourteen, then I started selling drugs to get $ for us. And that helped out a lot and allowed me to do most of what I needed to do, buy things and keep the lights on. And then I got told on for selling drugs, the police came and raided our house, I went to jail and we got evicted, I was sentenced as a juvenile. My sisters were taken away from my mother and put into the custody of relations. When I was in jail my father went to prison for four years and my mother got clean and has been clean ever since.*

*And when my father was coming home from his sentence, I was going in as an adult for this crime. He got right back into the same game he left and even to this day he's still out in the world smoking crack. He and my mother got divorced a couple of months after he was released and she wasn't doing drugs anymore and she got tired of him stealing from her to get crack. So now they live separate lives and my two little sisters are doing fine, working and have their own apartments.*

*I enjoyed the story of St Francis, it was very enlightening. I understood what you was saying and your reasons for not becoming a priest, you wanting a wife. Now tell me, don't you think that the wife you ended up with was worth it?! You know it's nothing wrong with you living by the same vows or code of one of the Franciscans, just modify things a little and add your wife into it. You know what you desire to do in your heart. You can be just as helpful as who you are now as you would have been if you stayed and became a priest. Do that make sense? In other words you don't have to be a professional hurley player to play the game of hurley. Thanks for your friendship and the time you spend reading my letters and responding to them.*

In 1998, Karla Faye Tucker was executed in Huntsville, Texas, for the murder in 1983 of Jerry Dean and Deborah Thornton. The extremely brutal murders followed a two-day orgy of sex, drugs and alcohol by Karla and her boyfriend. Karla Faye and her boyfriend were condemned to death for the murders. He died in prison; she became the first woman to be executed in Texas since the American Civil War.

At about sixteen years old, Karla Faye Tucker had moved in with Steven Griffith, whom she later married. They took care of the child of a friend for the five years they were together. When they separated, Karla took up prostitution and continued nearly up to the time of the murders. Karla Faye described her childhood in these words: 'I used to try and blame my mother because she was my role model and she fashioned and shaped me into what I was at an early age. She cheated on my father and got pregnant with me. This about destroyed my life and I was too young to know how to say that I was angry and hurt. My confusion and pain manifested itself in many ways. I often wonder why my mother never recognised that what she did to me affected me the way it did. At fourteen she took me to a place where there was all men and she wanted to "school me" in the art of being a call girl. I wanted to please my mother so much, I wanted her to be proud of me. So instead of saying no, I just tried to do what she asked. I did end up telling her I just couldn't be with all of those men because I didn't want to be doing prostitution. Her friends took me at fourteen and "schooled me" in the art of adult sex and with their warped and perverted sense of street values taught me that this was the thing to do to be respected and sought out in the "world we lived in". I was conditioned by the world my mother existed in.'

In prison, Karla Faye Tucker became a born-again Christian. She said 'Now God reigns in my heart and He fashions and shapes my beliefs and ideals and morals and scruples and values. The integrity of God and His Law now governs my life, my actions, my choices.'

Because of her conversion, her rehabilitation and her excellent disciplinary record while in prison, Karla Faye's supporters believed that she should be spared the death penalty. Others said that religious conversions for inmates are common and are not a legitimate basis for a pardon from the death penalty. Lawyers stressed that Karla Faye Tucker was fully rehabilitated and had demonstrated during her fourteen-year imprisonment that she posed no future threat to society.

Pleas for clemency came from all over the world – the UN commissioner on summary and arbitrary executions, the World Council of Churches, Pope John Paul II, Italian Prime Minister Romano Prodi, conservative US personalities Newt Gingrich and Pat Robertson, thousands of citizens, and the homicide detective who had recommended that she get the death penalty in the first place. There was even some support from her victims' siblings. Huntsville Prison's warden testified that she was a model prisoner and that, after fourteen years on death row, she had probably been reformed.

Tucker did not ask for a pardon or for freedom: she desired mercy from Texas in order to be able to spend the rest of her life in prison working in her ministry to inmates. Governor George W. Bush turned down her appeal. He could have indicated to the Texas Board of Pardons and Paroles that he wished the death sentence to be commuted, as he did in the case of Henry Lee Lucas. In that case, the Board gave him the decision he wanted, 17–1 in favour of commuting.

One journalist wrote that the 'worst single thing' he heard about George W. Bush had to do with this case. This story was widely reported. It was something Governor Bush said to a reporter in 1999 during his first presidential campaign. The reporter, conservative commentator Tucker Carlson, wrote as follows in *National Review*, a journal not known to be hostile toward Republicans: 'In the week before Tucker's execution, Bush says, Bianca Jagger and a number of other protesters came to Austin to demand clemency for Tucker.

"Did you meet with any of them?" I ask. Bush whips around and stares at me. "No, I didn't meet with any of them," he snaps, as though I've just asked the dumbest, most offensive question ever posed. "I didn't meet with Larry King either when he came down for it. I watched his interview with Tucker though. He asked her real difficult questions, like 'What would you say to Governor Bush?' " "What was her answer?" I wonder. "Please," Bush whimpers, his lips pursed in mock desperation, "don't kill me." '

The ugliness of a sitting governor mocking a prisoner's plea to spare her life horrified Carlson, especially after he looked up the transcript of Karla Faye Tucker's appearance on the TV programme *Larry King Live* and discovered that nowhere did it show the prisoner asking Bush to stay the execution.

What Bush said to Carlson was so obviously awful that he had no choice but to deny he had ever said it: 'Mr Carlson misread, mischaracterised me. He's a good reporter, he just misunderstood about how serious that was. I take the death penalty very seriously. I take each case seriously. I just felt he misjudged me. I think he misinterpreted my feelings. I know he did.'

A subsequent report, long after the election, that Laura Bush had dressed down her husband for his wisecrack to Carlson begs the question: why scold someone for something he never said?

Journalist Timothy Noah wrote in 2005: 'But then something peculiar happened. With the passage of time, reporters decided to forget the incident had ever happened. I can find no evidence that the anecdote has been reported during the past two years.' It's almost as though the press has decided that the story is too ugly to repeat.

Karla Faye Tucker selected five people, the maximum allowed, to be witnesses to her death. They included her husband and prison chaplain, Dana Brown, whom she had married in prison, and Ronald Carlson, the brother of Deborah Thornton, one of her victims. Ronald Carlson is opposed to all executions.

By the time Karla Faye climbed on to Texas's lethal-injection gurney, whispering 'Lord Jesus, help them to find my vein', people all over the world were praying for her. But Italian President Oscar Luigi Scalfaro noted in a public speech that spectators outside the Texas prison had cheered when Karla Faye Tucker was executed. 'And we are on the threshold of 2,000 years of Christ!' he exclaimed.

A Gospel singer's rendition of *Amazing Grace* was shouted down by cries of "Kill the bitch" from the crowd that gathered outside Huntsville prison. Proof, indeed, if proof were needed, that the death penalty damages far more people than those close to the victim and the perpetrator.

Many of those who support the death penalty claim that the use of mitigating circumstances by defence lawyers is part of a negative trend towards absolving individuals of personal responsibility. Tell that to people whose childhoods have been ravaged and destroyed by dysfunctional parents, by violence, by drugs. Knowledge of Karla Faye Tucker's drug-ridden childhood prostitution had been kept from the jury who sentenced her. Surely an informed jury would have found sufficient mitigating circumstances to spare her life? And how does one justify the execution of a fully rehabilitated woman who wanted nothing more than to continue her Christian ministry inside the prison walls? Retribution? Revenge?

*I have used drugs, I actually used drugs on the hour every hour. I smoked a lot of marujana from the age of fourteen until I was incarcerated. I was afraid to use the harder drugs that were out there, fear of not being able to control it and becoming dependent on it, so I stayed away from it. When I was younger I thought having a cigarette in your mouth was the coolest thing ever. I started smoking daily when I was around fifteen or sixteen, that's when I started buying cigarettes anyway and til this day I'm smoking them.*

*So you've never read anything from* Ralph Waldo Emerson. *I think it'll be best if you got* The Essential Writings of Ralph Waldo Emerson, *it'll give you a lot of his mind and thought process. Do you know that its writing was done in the 1800s, that's one of the reasons I was so intrigued with his work. Yes, we can read at night, we have lights in our cell that we operate ourselves.*

Dear Ray, The stories from your teens could have been straight from Claude Brown. Many thanks for asking Michael to send the book to me. It's lovely, it looks battered and well read. It must have been an eye-opener when it was first published. So far it is what I expected and I am not shocked by it – is that because I have read about poor USA life before or is it because I am getting dulled to the suffering of other people? Even though I can understand the book, I got a guide to it on the internet and like you, with Marsha Hunt's introduction, the guide is concentrating my mind, it picks out the theme of each chapter and discusses it. Like how Claude deals with his brother Pimp, how he tries to keep him out of trouble. Does Claude try hard enough or is he being influenced by his new 'middle-class outlook'? Near the end the chapters about the white girl, the Muslims, sorting out his brother Pimp, were very good. I thought Claude was a very clear writer, good pictures in simple language and mostly done through dialogue – that takes some doing. I think the book got better as it went on. I saw on the internet that Claude Brown died in 2002 from 'respiratory failure', he was sixty-five.

In the '60s and '70s in Dublin young people in poorer areas went straight on to heroin – I think that's unusual – great sadness and misery followed for them. I see by the newspapers that cocaine is now the most common drug here and that it is being used, usually snorted, by people from all social classes. The police make huge drug seizures every day but it is making no difference, the drug is still flooding in from places like Colombia in south America. . . . Lots of it comes to Dublin, which has a quarter of the population of the country, and then the rest goes to smaller towns around the country – some people say every village in Ireland is being affected by drug use – as you get older and live in a respectable suburban area, lots of these things pass you by – I was much more clued in when I was working with a homeless group, the Simon Community, when I was younger.

I would be scared to try drugs. . . . I smoked ordinary cigarettes from age eleven to thirty-eight! Even now, after being off cigarettes for years, I would be terrified to take even one pull of a cigarette in case I got addicted again. I think it is easier for some people to become addicted – I might be one of those!

# 6

# Friends and Family

*Michael told me that you and he had exchanged e-mails. As I told you already, he was my first penfriend and he's been a very loyal and reliable friend to me. I honestly think he was my first true friend that accepted me for who I was.*

*What you said in your last letter made me think back to school when I thought the days were so long, I often wondered if the school clocks worked! I've always been one to like the females and I thought back to the days I was trying to impress, cleaning my shoes and ironing my clothes the night before. I had a crush on this girl and I used to stand in front of her locker before school just to open it for her. When I got older we went out, courted for a while. I was no longer in school, she continued with her education, then she went off to college out of the state, we lost contact. When I saw her again, she had a child and was living back in town, had been for a year or so. We picked up the pieces and became what we young people here call 'Friends with Benefits'.*

*The handball alley you spoke of that was a gathering point sounded like a spot we used to meet at after school, sometimes during school when we were 'shooting hooky'. We used to call that the Honey Comb Hideout. And we had another spot we used to hang out at that was a laundry mat and another that was a bowling alley, but the bowling alley sometimes called the school officials when students came to the alley during school hours so we stopped hanging out there. But it was good while it lasted!*

The past couple of days have been very cold so I just stayed in and read – a pleasure and a luxury. I didn't even watch television. I read one very good book by an Irish-language poet, Cathal Ó Searcaigh, who wrote about the time he spends every year in Nepal near Mount Everest. There were great pictures in it, another world. There are lots of different worlds all over the world.

Soon now the days will be getting longer here and they say that after 1 February, the feast of St Brigid, one of the patrons of Ireland, each day gets longer by a *coiscéim coiligh* – Irish for 'a cockerel's step'! But only the older people know those kind of sayings.

St Brigid – not sure whether she really existed or not, she may have been a Christian form of a pagan goddess – wanted land to build a monastery on but at first the king refused to give her any land at all. Eventually he laughed and said, 'You can have as much land as your cloak will cover.'

She put her cloak on the ground and it spread and spread and spread and spread (!) until she had enough land to build her convent. This all happened about 1,500 years ago. The convent became famous and people from all over Ireland came to it to pray and to ask for advice. Brigid was very advanced for the time and said that men and women were equal. Today a peace group in Ireland holds a conference around the feast of St Brigid every year and brings famous speakers to talk at it – so the fame of St Brigid lives on. Brigid, or the Irish form, Bríd, is still a common name in Ireland.

A custom that is still alive is to make a St Brigid's Cross from reeds every year and put it over the door for protection. We have one at the front door but it's been there for a good few years – we should make a new one!

* * *

*I think the problem with my back comes from all the pushing and bumping on the basketball court, combined with those uneven uncomfortable mattresses we are given. My biggest problem is staying off the basketball court when I'm injured, I hate to stand around and watch a good game . . . sometimes I take pain pills thirty minutes before going out so my back wouldn't hurt but I pay for that when I get back in!*

*You get a lot of action looking out your kitchen window. The way you explained about the sparrow hawk swooping down on the little bird put me in mind of the wildlife specials on TV. I enjoy the wildlife shows. The pigeon getting killed by the cat, magpies trying to eat the peanuts from the feeders and suburban foxes getting killed by cars – that makes me think of all the people and friends I've had growing up that was killed trying to survive and feed their families in the streets. How or why that thought occurred, I really don't know, it just came into my mind.*

*I enjoy your letters very much. Thanks for befriending me and letting me escape to Ireland, I enjoy the trips. I did tell my mom and sisters my new friend from Ireland said 'Hi'. They all except my mom said 'Who's that?' My mom said 'Hi' back and then she asked the question, who are you? My sisters did the opposite! They asked first and then said 'Hi' back!*

*I'm glad you are getting to know Michael through the e-mails. Yes, Michael is a very good and honest friend and has been for many years. I remember when he first wrote, I was a year in on death row and new to penfriends. He wrote and I was hesitant to write back, in fear of what people in the mailroom or other inmates would think if I wrote to a gay guy. I called my mom and was like 'This gay guy wrote me, do you think I should write back?' and she was like 'Do you have a problems with gays? No! Then write back.' And I'm very glad I did.*

We had a nice few days painting Catherine and Martin's house down in County Clare – just one room with high ceilings for a start. It needed two coats, hadn't been painted for a while. I did the high-up painting, Bríd held the paint pot. When I began to tire on the second day, Catherine did some of the lower-down painting and Martin was in charge of food. He is a really good cook, he lived for five years in Italy and learned a lot there.

We didn't fight or even argue once, it was too hot! The only excitement was once when I was on top of the ladder high up – it started to slip down the wall and the foot of it slid along the floor. Bríd said 'Oh Jesus' and dropped the paint. She must have meant the 'Oh Jesus' to be a prayer because the ladder stopped again after sliding a few feet. That was the only excitement. In the two days we were painting, about ten cars, maximum, passed down the road . . . I said, this would suit Ray perfectly!

Another day when Catherine and Martin were out I painted a bedroom – a nice primrose colour. The room wasn't too big and I don't mind painting once I get started and once I have somebody to clean the splashes. Bríd in this case! Then when they came back Catherine went into the room and was in there a couple of minutes before she noticed the change. That hurt!

I'm enclosing a few photos and postcards. Six is the most you can receive? I hope I'm right. You'll recognise Mr Fox – one night just as it was getting dark we were looking out over the fields when Bríd spotted a fox heading off across the fields with his long tail stretched out behind him. It seems that they take more or less the same route every day and at the same time every day in their search for food. Catherine and Martin's two hens are still surviving but it's a constant worry!

And yet another bit of news from Clare. Catherine was walking up the road the other day, she saw Woody, the dog, eyeing her, then Woody ran and she ran after him, she suspected what he was up to . . . and she caught up with him just as he was about to eat an egg one of the hens had laid under a bush! She had been wondering why the hens didn't seem to be laying! They'll have to get a way to stop the hens laying outside. She said Woody's coat is sleek – from the protein in the eggs! As I say, a constant worry!

*The visit with my family went fine, very pleasant. I went out around 10AM and stayed out until the visit was over, which was 2.30 PM. We laughed a lot, ate a lot, played a lot and talked a lot, we pretty much just had a good time. St Patrick's Day is a very recognised day over here, everyone wears the colour green, my mother had a green shirt on and my daughter had it in her hair pins. She told me if you don't wear green, you're supposed to get pinched so she went around the tables and pinched everyone without green on. So wrapped up in a nutshell that's what went down on the visiting yard during my visit.*

*It sounded like Catherine really put you to work painting her house. I'm sure you didn't have a problem with doing the work, what father wouldn't get great pleasure out of that type of work. I pray, someday I'll get that same job, or any job for that matter, from my daughter and that I'll be able to do 'hard labor' for her.*

*The postcards and photos you sent were beautiful. I would like to visit the Burren, it not only looks like a nice place but it also sounds like an interesting place. Catherine and Martin, I would imagine, visit Poulnabrone a lot or maybe they've become used to it by now, right? I've never saw or heard of a ring fort so the things you told me concerning them were new to me. There's a lot of historic things in Clare like that church and the Celtic Cross, I wasn't familiar with them at all. That's one thing I like about corresponding with you, it's like I get educated on something every letter.*

*But I really don't like staying in places too quiet. My grandmother's house was similar to how Catherine and Martin's house is, the surrounding and all. When I was younger and stayed at her house, it got boring very fast and you had to walk too far to get to the next house to find other kids to play with. Now I guess I'm what you'd call a city slicker, opposite to being a country boy! I'm looking at the view from the back of their house and I don't see anything but green grass fields, lots of it. No, that mightn't suit me at all, you could hear yourself thinking out there.*

*P.S. This guy you mentioned in your letter, Gerry Adams, I've never heard of.*

Thanks, Ray, for the photos of you in your cell, I got some copies made and am enclosing them. Where I get the photos copied, I could see that the man was curious, so I told him where you were. He was amazed and very appalled too by the death penalty. He thinks your 'friend' – I must stop calling him your friend – George W. is 'slightly' mad and dangerous because he thinks he has a direct line to God. This man is sixty, as thin as a rake and takes part in international athletic competitions for older people. A great man for a chat – it took a long time to get your photos copied!

I thought I'd wait until I was back home to tell you that I was in hospital for three nights, they were trying to make my heartbeat regular by medication. I thought I'd read a few books but it seemed a bit unfriendly to be stuck in a book all the time when there are three other people in the ward and would you believe it, one of them was a woman! Each of the four of us had something wrong with our hearts but there were only two monitors in that part of the hospital so we were all put in together in case we needed a monitor. We didn't! We got on fine – with a woman in the ward there were no blue jokes and no endless talk about football. A couple of years ago I spent a week in a ward with five very nice guys but they talked soccer from waking up to going to sleep and had heated arguments about it. I read a lot that time!

Anyway, they put me on the treadmill for a stress test – and they speed it up gradually and make it steeper. They took me off after 5 minutes 29 seconds. I saw it on the monitor, I was disgusted! Two other men in the ward with heart problems did over ten minutes on it, they were boasting about it! The only boasting I could do was to say that I knew a fellow who could stay on it forever. That was you! Hope you don't mind. But five miserable minutes!

Cathal is almost walking, trying to get into the fireplace and succeeding once in getting into the dishwasher! Catherine was in Minsk in Belarus as part of her work. They gave advice and equipment to an orphanage for disabled children. Last year, or two years ago maybe, she found it depressing, but this time the people in charge seem to have benefited from the help and advice. The people working there were more cheerful themselves and more confident, and that rubbed off on the children. The orphanage had also been painted, the children were getting out of bed – last time they stayed in bed all day long and in some more difficult cases they were even tied to the bed. This time the children seemed happier and now they know how to play with toys – last time they didn't know how to play at all. So she came back to County Clare in good form.

* * *

*Thanks for the compliments concerning my writing. I have wrote somewhat of a life story a couple of years ago for my attorney, they wanted me to just write out different memories about my life that was defining. I tried keeping a prison diary, it didn't last more than three days, I don't know, those type of things I just find more stressful, having to sit down and write like that strictly for the purpose of reading it later.*

*I do think I have a very dedicated and smart attorney, the best I've had since I've been incarcerated and certainly as good as I can get without having to pay. I have a lot of faith in him getting me a new trial which is better than anything, well, not freedom but it's close. He thought my little autobio was sad and happy and another word he used that I can't think of right now. He stated he had a lot of mixed emotions that was for the most part uplifting to see me still surviving mentally.*

*You really made me laugh out loud when you said your granddaughter, Róisín, has taken up Irish dancing and likes to show off her steps. 'Watch me dancing' is what she says and you are stuck with a thirty-minute show! I have seen many do the traditional Irish dance on TV, isn't it called* River Dance, *at least that's what we call it over here.*

*I'm sending you some Irish jokes that I got from Michael. His mother comes from a place called Cavan. Here's one joke. Paddy was driving down a street in a sweat because he had an important meeting and couldn't find a parking place. Looking up to heaven, he said, 'Lord, take pity on me. If you find me a parking place, I will go to Mass every Sunday for the rest of me life and give up me Irish whiskey.' Miraculously a parking place appeared. Paddy looked up again and said, 'Never mind, I found one.'*

*Some news – I've been in court in my home town and all in all it was a positive step into a good direction for my appeals. I'm not sure if I can explain this as well as I should but I had a week in the hometown, got to see some of my family and got a couple of visits from my father so that was good. Overall, I enjoyed the visit and the three-hour trip there and back. I hadn't been home for two years and it's amazing how much could be built and changed in that time.*

Eighteen-year-old Jeremy Gross was, without any doubt, guilty of the most brutal murder of convenience-store cashier Christopher Beers in Indianapolis, Indiana. In August 1998, the shooting and the last moments of Beers' life were caught on four cameras.

The prosecutor was confident that any jury in the world would recommend the ultimate penalty in this case. It seemed obvious that the 'death qualified' jury – a strange phrase, in capital cases jurors opposed to the death penalty are disqualified – would vote for the death penalty.

Bob Hill (47) defended Gross. He was an experienced, skilful lawyer who had already defended fourteen other men facing the death penalty. From the start he conceded that Gross had no case: he – not the prosecutor – showed the video evidence to the jury. For the next five days, forty-one witnesses described the young life of Jeremy Gross. Drink, drugs, extreme domestic violence, twenty-seven addresses where Gross had lived in his first sixteen years and thirty-three schools he had attended. The horrific details of Gross's childhood brought tears to the eyes of many of the jurors, but Hill knew that it could defeat his purpose if he merely described Gross as an abused and broken youth. If the jury decided that Gross was too far gone, they might just decide to end the useless life of such a miserable person.

Hill found the foster parents who for one year rescued Jeremy, when he was eight, and his sister. They gave them love and kindness, gave them chores to do, gave them attention, gave them the status of true family members. Jeremy joined the Scouts, began to do well at school, played Little League baseball. All through his trial, Jeremy made eye contact with just one person, his foster father, who could hardly speak as he told how he and his wife wanted to adopt the two children but were prevented by social services, who returned the children to their abusive mother.

Hill said that he wanted the jurors to walk in the shoes of Jeremy Gross. He succeeded in persuading the jury that there was something in Jeremy Gross that was worth saving. They voted unanimously that Jeremy should live. Hill had spent eighteen months preparing his defence case. Bob Hill is an unusual and exceptional defence lawyer but his committed and methodical approach must become the norm if the death-penalty system is to be reformed. In January 2007, there were twenty-three people on death row in Indiana.

In the state of Colorado, the defence in capital cases is taken very seriously – in January 2007, there were just two people on death row in Colorado. The Office of the State Public Defender lobbies for funding from the legislature in order to have a high and uniform standard of defence across the State. The Office trains defence attorneys and hires only lawyers who want a career in public defence. Here defence lawyers do not put all their efforts into the 'guilty or not guilty' phase of a trial. The sentencing phase is crucial, it means the difference between life and death, and needs just as much expertise, knowledge and commitment from defence attorneys. The sentencing phase of a trial came to the fore in the 1970s and highlighted the need for trained and committed defence lawyers.

As the civil-rights movement grew in the US, crime seemed manageable, and in 1957, for the first time, support for the death penalty fell below 50 percent. In 1972, the US Supreme Court (*Furman* v. *Georgia*) stated that the death penalty was 'not inconsistent with our respect for the dignity of man' and in its ruling it avoided the issue of racism. However, it ruled that the death penalty was unconstitutional because of its 'random and capricious' application; it was, therefore, a 'cruel and unusual' punishment and in violation of amendments to the US Constitution. Over six hundred death-row prisoners had their sentences commuted.

In 1976, the Supreme Court (*Gregg* v. *Georgia*) reinstated the death penalty and laid out reforms to eliminate the arbitrary application of the death penalty. But Sr Helen Prejean claims that 'the unpredictable way the death penalty is imposed today is as arbitrary as it was when the Supreme Court declared it unconstitutional'.

The 1976 judgement provided for two-stage trials with separate jury deliberations. At the end of the first stage, the jury pronounces the defendant's guilt or innocence; in the second stage, the jury or the judge determines the sentence. The court judgement also approved automatic review of conviction and sentence. This was the end of the four-year moratorium on the death penalty. The death penalty swung into action again in January 1977 with the execution of Gary Gilmore in Utah.

You asked about writing. The only piece I had published in English recently, Ray, was about time and change, in a way something like you saw on your trip to your home town. 'The Day I Tangled with Tom Clifford' was the title. . . . Explanatory notes are in brackets! Here it is.

> I like to dream that I might have had a career in sport. I also like to delude myself that I have a fairly good sporting pedigree. From the age of thirteen to eighteen, I spent my time chasing a Gaelic football and for my efforts I won a prestigious medal. And then a weakness in my knee put an end to what was to have been an illustrious sporting career.
>
> Just as well maybe but sometimes I think I might have done better if one of those blonde-ponytailed physios that I see on TV, running on to the pitch to attend to fallen heroes, had been around when my knee crumpled under me every time I landed after jumping for the ball.
>
> But in those days, blondes – not to mind the ones with ponytails – were not that common, it was after all the era of the comely maidens. (Éamon de Valera, who fought in 1916 and became President of Ireland, used to say that he longed for the day when we could return to the simple Ireland of comely maidens dancing at the crossroads. No chance!) Anyway, the long and the short of it was that there was no help to be had for my poor knee!
>
> Before my short sporting career took off, I had confined myself to going to soccer matches at Turner's Cross and rugby matches in Musgrave Park. In those days in Cork, I never had the money to pay into Turner's Cross but had to wait for half-time when the gates were opened wide to admit everyone still outside free of charge.
>
> Actually, I didn't have the money to get into Musgrave Park either. Luckily for us, those were innocent days when PR and corporate image were unheard of, days when it was easy for young fellas to duck under the fence and through the hedge. Respectable adults, whose sons attended the two rugby-playing schools in the city, couldn't be seen doing that and so they

paid at the turnstile. Fair enough, I thought, if they have the money they might as well subsidise those of us who had very little of it.

In the late '40s, I saw many great players in Musgrave Park – Ernie O'Keeffe, Bertie O'Hanlon, Mick Lane and the others who helped Ireland to Triple Crown glory, (The Triple Crown was a contest in rugby between Ireland, England, Scotland and Wales – still fiercely contested.)

In those days we depended for the sports news on the wireless, where the pictures were allegedly better. Now when I see players on television passing comments to the referee and when you don't need to be a lip reader to figure out what they're saying, I think back to the muddy day in Musgrave Park when the scrum broke up and an impressive expletive escaped the lips of a large and angry forward. Immediately he received a sharpish slap on the face from his captain, with the warning that we wanted none of that kind of thing here. I know it's hard to believe but I saw it happening right there in front of me.

A certain frisson of excitement would be in the Cork air the week before a match against one of the Limerick teams, Garryowen or Young Munster. Those guys in pale blue with the white star of Garryowen or the yellow and black of Young Munster brought their own brand of tough rugby and the crowds flocked to see them.

When Young Munster came, Tom Clifford came. He was the working-class man, he worked on the docks (your typical rugby player usually works in insurance, finance or medicine, and so on). Clifford proved, it was said, that rugby was a game for every class. He was fearless, he was indomitable, he was battle scarred, he was like a tank, he was huge . . . and I wanted his autograph. I looked up at him, craning my neck.

'Could I have your autograph . . . please,' I squeaked.

He kept walking to the dressing room. I asked again in a slightly louder squeak. He kept on walking. I thought of tapping him on the knee or I might even reach his thigh. Instead I squeaked again. Thump! I landed on the ground, I was sore.

'Sorry, young fella,' said Tom. 'I didn't see you there.' And he lifted me off the ground with one hand. 'Sure, I'll give you my autograph.'

'Thanks,' I squeaked and limped off. And that was the start of the weakness in my knee. It has never been quite the same since!

That's it! Looking forward to hearing from you, Ray. How is Rachel, your Mom and your sisters? Any news from them since the visit – how have they been since?

* * *

*Did the saying turn out to be correct this March – did it go out like a lamb? Hope your grandson, Cathal, is recovering from his cold – you called him a 'tiny scrap'. I may start calling some of the smaller guys here 'Tiny Scrap'!*

*You know what you said about the time you was 12–13 years old and having little fights with the boys from the next street over? I grew up like that also but the difference was our fights sometimes got bad and escalated to weapons like knives and guns and that's how the gangs and the turf wars were started. As a matter of fact I have a tattoo of the district I was ready to die and kill for as a young'un. Young feisty boys trying to let it be known who is the baddest and who wants respect on their street or in their neighborhood, that's the start of it, that's real talk and that's the start of the pain.*

*I will pass the address you sent for* Lifelines Ireland *to some of the guys I know is in search of pen pals. You all take care and know you're thought of and greatly appreciated.*

* * *

*I've just been maintaining [coping], it's getting hot here, I write letters at night when it's cooler. You said Catherine and Martin have planted some apple trees and have at last put up a run for the hens. They're coming along very well with getting used to country life. My grandfather used to have hens when I was younger, I used to run around and chase them in the yard. I used to like to hear their wings flap when I scared them.*

*You're really opposed to wars. Fresh out of hospital, you went to the anti-war march. Don't think I would have been able to do that, not that I agree with war, but not fresh out of surgery. Yes, George W. is falling in the popular contest. Hopefully he'll be impeached out of office before his three years are up. After all the hell was raised about Clinton getting sexual favors in the White House, how is it all Bush is doing is accepted? I think his misjudgements are far greater than what Clinton's were. What do you think?*

*I enjoyed what you said about sneaking into Turner's Cross and Musgrave Park. That made me think back to when I used climb the gates to sneak into football games. And we used run through the movie theatre doors, imagine about ten teenagers running through one door at the same time! Best not to tell your grandson, Eoin!*

*No, you won't be able to send* Manchild in a Promised Land *back to me. I sent it to you because it's something I wanted you to have and I wanted you to add it to your collection of books. And that one book, whenever it's read or talked about, you'll be able to say my friend in the US sent me this book as a gift. . . .*

*P.S. Was Róisín doing the can-can when she came back from the family trip to Paris?!*

# 7

# We're All Doing Time

A sleeping lawyer and George W.! A joke that does the rounds among defence lawyers in capital murder cases is that courts accept the effectiveness of any lawyer who can pass the mirror test: hold a mirror under a lawyer's nose, and if there are signs of breath, then, say the courts, you have a lawyer!

In the state of Texas in 1983, Calvin Burdine was tried for the murder of his gay partner, W. T. Wise. He asserted his innocence and claimed that Douglas McCreight, who was to be his accomplice in the robbing of Wise's money, was the guilty one. McCreight pleaded guilty and was released on parole after eight years. Burdine pleaded not guilty and was sentenced to death. Arbitrary justice? A disgustingly low point was reached in the trial when the prosecutor urged the jury to condemn Burdine to death as it was no punishment to send a homosexual to prison, it was like letting a child loose in a sweet shop. The judge allowed the prosecutor to use the word 'faggot' throughout the trial.

Several witnesses saw Burdine's court-appointed attorney, Joe Frank Cannon, dozing repeatedly during the trial, once for as long as ten minutes. He had almost no notes on the case, his questioning of witnesses was totally inadequate. Some lawyers who tried to defend Cannon argued that maybe he only slept during boring parts of the evidence! Ten other clients of Joe Frank Cannon were also condemned to death. In Texas almost a third of the lawyers who represented clients condemned to death have been disciplined for legal misbehaviour. Nevertheless, the courts upheld Burdine's conviction; one assistant solicitor-general argued that a sleeping lawyer is no different from a lawyer under the influence of drink or drugs, no different from a lawyer with Alzheimer's or a lawyer with mental illness – all of those lawyers had already been declared by various courts to be 'not ineffective'.

The execution of Burdine was stayed five times and eventually, in a narrow 2–1 decision, the Fifth Circuit court held that Calvin Burdine had not received adequate representation. His conviction was overturned and a retrial ordered. In 2003 the prosecution offered a deal. Burdine had to plead guilty to capital murder, aggravated assault and possession of a weapon. There would be no long trial, no death penalty. His lawyers advised him to take the deal. What else could he do? He had no money to hire expert attorneys. He was sentenced to three consecutive life terms. He may be innocent.

The case of the sleeping lawyer hit the headlines and was even debated during the Bush-Gore presidential campaign. When the then governor of Texas, George W. Bush, who presided over the execution of 152 prisoners, was asked about the sleeping lawyer, he chuckled. Mr Bush has never conceded that even one prisoner on death row in Texas might have been wrongfully convicted.

* * *

*My birthday was really just another day, I went out and played basketball, came back, fixed me a birthday meal and that was pretty much the day. The food here is okay, it's nothing to call home about but with the right seasoning it could be eaten. I rarely eat it myself, I buy food off the store with the funds I get from friends. I received lots of cards from family and friends which I enjoyed, so the mail was the highlight of that birthday.*

*I was intending to write you earlier tonight but I fell asleep and I'm just waking up. Mail goes out in an hour and I want to get this letter to you tonight so forgive my handwriting if it starts to get bad. I do a lot of writing during these early hours, it be quieter so I sleep in the daytime and get up when the sun is gone down and vice versa in the winter. I was pleased you liked the photos I sent from outside of my cell. I used live upstairs with a view of lights and a prison yard. Now I'm downstairs. Those lights outside the cells are safety lights, they never go off, the one in front of my cell stays on 365 days a year. Some guys hit it really hard with a broom handle without breaking the light cover. I used to do that. Now I just put a towel in front of my door to block out the light.*

*The scene here at night is quiet but there's always someone up and awake. When I woke up just now my head was hurting. I'm fine now but the headaches come and go. I take aspirin to knock the aching away and then lay low, that usually works. You said you rarely get headaches, wish I could say that!*

You remember the court case about the Pitstop Ploughshares, the five who damaged a US warplane in Shannon Airport so that it couldn't be used in Iraq? They were found not guilty! They never denied that they did the damage but they claimed they had a 'sufficient excuse' when you think of the damage one warplane can do. They are very religious and so I think the main anti-war groups stayed out of this, which is a pity really. After damaging the plane, they knelt down and prayed until the police came to arrest them.

The judge, a woman this time, was very fair, I think, and a turning point was when she allowed witnesses to be called who described the destruction in Iraq and also allowed them to argue that they had 'just cause' and that their actions were justified in order to prevent death.

Some of the Irish government and the US embassy here were annoyed at the decision. At the end of the trial one member of the jury was heard saying: 'You might only get one chance to do something good in life and for me today was it.' The five started to cry when the verdict was announced. During the three trials, two mistrials, I helped hand out leaflets a couple of days in support of the five – almost everybody was friendly except one fellow in a van who shouted over: 'You waster – get a job!'

Did you ever feel like making a rude gesture, Ray? Thing is I don't know any rude gestures! And if you believe that . . . !

The oldest of the protesters, forty-six-year-old Australian Ciaron O'Reilly, said the jury's verdict was a setback for the government policy of allowing US troops to use Shannon Airport. 'We're delighted that the conscience of the community – twelve people selected off the streets of Dublin – has spoken unanimously in acquitting us, and it really sends a strong message to the Irish government that they have no popular mandate for what they are doing in Shannon,' he said. I think he was being very optimistic there.

* * *

*When you write, fold your letters down like I did mine. When the letter is the same size as the envelope, it gets cut in half when they open the letters in the mailroom. You got to fold the letter lower like I did this letter. Thanks for sending me the info on Darfur. I saw the whole thing on TV and already knew some of these things. It's sad what's going on over there.*

*I haven't talked to my family for a while over the phone. The phone bill is kind of expensive and my mother can't afford to talk to me but once or twice a month. I sometimes lose track of that and call too much. So now the phone has been disconnected for a while until my mother can work out the funds. So with that going on, we write.*

Bríd and myself are going to Cape Clear, a small island off the south-west corner of Ireland, for three weeks. I probably told you about this island – we have been going there for over twenty years and I was there for the first time in 1961 when there was no electricity there and the usual dinner was mackerel and potatoes – day after day! It is just your kind of place (!), very remote, small – about two miles by one mile, only 120 people living there all year round, a small farming, fishing, partly Irish-speaking community. One church, two pubs – three in the summer season. We are renting a house there. It is pure escapism, we are so lucky. We know all the people there by now – it's the kind of place where they know everything about you and you know everything about them! Life can be hard there at times and sometimes they have rows but then they know they have to live together so they start all over again to get on with each other. We don't do anything there except walk around and sit on the harbour wall and talk and we come back with all kinds of useless – to us! – information about fishing, cattle, weather, the sea, dolphins and whales, the tides. . . . Even if there is no sun we will be burnt by the wind and the top of my poor bald head will suffer!

* * *

*I understood what you was saying about your hand shaking not allowing you write a long-hand letter like those I write. Typing is fine. I'm sorry about laughing. Well, actually I wasn't laughing* at *you when you told me about the tea jumping from your cup to your forehead, I was laughing* with *you!*

*Thanks for sending the history of the Navajo code-breakers in World War 2 but honestly I didn't find it that interesting, sorry. I enjoyed looking at the postcard with Mr Fox on the front. It states on the back that they are rarely seen out in the daylight, I didn't know they were so plentiful in Ireland. You say they travel the same route every day at the same time searching for food. I didn't know that, I didn't think they were that predictable. Thanks for the postcard from Clare of the Cliffs of Moher. That's a beautiful view, something I would like to experience for myself. It looks very peaceful standing atop of the cliff, I bet a lot of thinking has taken place there for many people.*

*Yes, we have our own support group among friends, it's difficult to live with someone in such confinement and not develop friendships. So we do turn to each other for support during a tough day.*

*I was pleased to get the news on the five who was charged with damaging the US warplane in Shannon being found not guilty. I can imagine how annoyed the powers that be were with the final outcome of the trial. You said they cried as the verdict was read – those were tears of joy and relief. You know, I was wondering how is it that €2.5m in damage was done by the protestors. What did they ram the plane with – a bulldozer a few times? As they very well should have!*

We came back to Dublin a week earlier than we had planned but that is a long story! You will hardly believe what I'm going to tell you, Ray!

Our friend, Rahim, and about forty other asylum-seekers from Afghanistan, went on hunger strike! On 14 May they moved into St Patrick's Cathedral, a big old Protestant church in the middle of Dublin. They went in one by one casually and then they gathered inside and told the cathedral people that they were looking for sanctuary. Long ago you could look for sanctuary or refuge in churches but I don't think the law recognises that now.

They wanted their claims for asylum to be heard and they wanted to stay here – they are terrified to go back home. The Department of Justice and the government here have warned Irish people not to go to Afghanistan for safety reasons so they can't very well deport people to Afghanistan. At the same time they don't want to give Rahim and the others permission to stay here – so they drag everything out and in some cases it is taking years for people to get a decision on their asylum claim.

Then stories started to leak to the papers, from the Department of Justice maybe? It said in lots of papers that Rahim's uncle was in the Taliban, which is true, but they never reported that the uncle actually resisted the Taliban and suffered for it.

There seemed to be a kind of media campaign to demonise the hunger strikers.

After a day or two they went on thirst strike as well – this affected them very quickly and some of them had to be brought to hospital because they were dehydrated. Rahim was one of them, he also had chest pains. One of the women doctors used start to cry every time she saw them being brought in and Rahim had to say: 'Please, doctor, don't cry or we will all start crying.'

Supporters had brought them sleeping bags and so on but another crowd also gathered outside the church shouting: 'Throw them out . . . go home . . . lock them up', so for a while it was quite ugly. Rahim was one of the spokesmen and he told us that he was exhausted from dealing with the media, TV stations from all over the world. His sister in Afghanistan saw him on TV and phoned him frantic with worry – he assured her he was only a spokesman and was not on hunger strike at all! She believed him.

The Department of Justice then refused to let those who were brought to hospital back into the cathedral again and didn't allow doctors to put drips into the men in the cathedral – I don't know if they had the right to do that but they did it anyway. The Department also stopped the cathedral priests from negotiating a compromise settlement. So gradually they broke down the resistance and the strike ended after a week. The men were brought to court yesterday and the case was adjourned for a few weeks. The cathedral people have not made any complaint or charge so it's up to the police now

Rahim's friend, Hamid, didn't go on strike, I don't think he agreed with it but he said that he ate so little during that week that he might as well have been on hunger strike! I think the whole thing showed how isolated the Afghans are here.

So there we were down on our remote island – no newspapers – wondering what to do! We sent text messages to Rahim to try to encourage him but he hadn't the energy to reply. We told a few people that we knew one of the men on hunger strike and the word spread like wildfire! So we had to answer lots of questions and in the end we were glad we didn't come to Dublin to be outside the cathedral because we were able to tell the people on Cape Clear something about asylum-seekers – many thought they were just the same as any other foreigner, so we were able to tell them about the lives of asylum-seekers, how Ireland and Denmark are the only two European countries that don't allow asylum-seekers to work, about the bad effects of poor food and accommodation and so on.

When we came back, the strike was over and Rahim was recovering – they were depending on a voluntary group to help them with medical advice, no help from the Department of Justice. On Tuesday, Rahim and Hamid came out to us and we were sitting around talking and having a cup of tea when Sky News rang Rahim – ten minutes later a reporter arrived and did a short interview at our kitchen table with a brief shot of myself and Bríd. Good job I painted the kitchen last year! I bet you never expected that story!

Apart from that, we had a lovely time in Cape Clear. The weather wasn't great but there are great walks there, always uphill – no matter where you go, you can't avoid hills – but there were great views over the sea and the mainland. We are going there for about twenty-four years now so we know all the people. Some are getting old and we visited one or two of them and most nights other people would call in to the house we were staying in and we used have great chats about everything and anything and very often you'd learn lots about various interesting things that you'd never talk about in the city.

Catherine came down to see us one weekend. Seán, a friend in Cape Clear, wanted to give her four goslings when he heard what a 'farmer' she was turning into! She refused – politely – goslings are one thing but grown geese are another! They would probably eat up Woody, the dog, who by the way has calmed down and is no longer chasing after the two hens!

*Some days it's tiresome when you wake up and be like 'this again . . . and again', the routine things that are repeated over and over by us all. Other days one is happy to wake up, those are the days that something is looked forward to. I have good days and bad days, I usually just lie on the bed on the bad ones and watch the walls, count the bars and think how or what have I got myself into. I don't usually share those days with you in letters because if I'm having a bad depressing day, I don't write. And when it's over and I do write, it's not something I dwell on so it never comes out in the letter. But, yes, this place is truly an emotional roller coaster but what's new in life?! I hate this place. I wanted to leave here the moment I got here but what can I do, what can you do about that? Neither of us can do anything so there's no need for me to depress myself or burden you with my feelings on that ugly side of this place. So I tend to spare you the details. Do that make sense? Well, that's some inside info I wanted to say, just so you'll have a better understanding of what this place can do to you. I could go on for pages but I'd rather not bore you nor sadden you with that. . . . I liked the postcard of the stonechat bird. It's a nice picture.*

*CALLING ALL BETS*

*Confined to a cage*
*for the rest of my life*
*forever in loneliness*
*living in strife.*
*Nothing else matters*

*escape is my goal,*
*it's mounted and planted*
*deep in my soul.*

*The risks are irrelevant*
*especially for me*
*if I make it I win*
*if I die then I'm free.*
*So let the chips fall*
*I'll have no regrets,*
*the stakes are my life*
*but I'm callin' all bets.*

*Now some might think I'm crazy*
*and well . . . I might just be*
*but I'm tired of livin'*
*if I can't be free.*

'I spent nine years, one month and seventeen days in the penal system. I'm part of Illinois' exonerated. I was released from death row, but I'm not free of death row. Death row is hell, and so is my life like hell. I have not been compensated. Death row lives within me today. It's alive – the pain, the hurt. Every day is a day of bad memories. I cannot forget death row. I cannot forget the people who manufactured the lies and manufactured a case against me.

'George Ryan concluded his tenure as Illinois governor in the most dramatic fashion in the entire history of governors. Governor Ryan issued a blanket commutation for everyone in prison who was under the death penalty. For those of us who believed that the death penalty should be abolished, we praised to the highest and celebrated. And for those who supported the death penalty, many screamed in anger and resentment. God used Governor Ryan to save lives and wipe the bloodstains of men from the judicial system.

'Abolition of the death penalty will follow, and the system will be changed forever. It's time to abolish the death penalty. The time is now. The death penalty cannot be cleared up. It is dead wrong. It is too final.'

These words were spoken by convicted death-row prisoner Darby Tillis in 2001 after receiving a pardon based on actual innocence from Illinois governor George Ryan. Tillis and Perry Cobb were wrongly convicted and sentenced to death for the 1977 murder of two white men during an armed robbery on Chicago's northside. They are the only people in US history to be tried five times. The first two trials ended in hung juries, but the third resulted in convictions and death sentences. The Illinois Supreme Court reversed this conviction, they were then tried two more times before being acquitted in 1987. By then it was clear that false eyewitness statements had been made against them.

George Ryan (74) was the Republican governor of Illinois from 1999 to 2001. He greatly improved the Illinois highway system and public transport, gave record funding to education, was the first sitting US governor to meet Fidel Castro, and became known across the country when he raised the national debate on capital punishment. Some people suspected that his work on death-penalty issues was used to divert attention from looming political scandals. He retired from politics in 2003 and was convicted on corruption charges in 2006. As of June 2008, he is serving six years and six months in a federal correctional institution in Indiana.

The current governor of Illinois is Rod R. Blagojevich (51, Democrat). He is the second Serbian-American to be elected a state governor. He favours gun control and supports a moratorium on the execution of death-row prisoners, even though no such executions are likely to occur for years, since George Ryan commuted all death sentences in Illinois shortly before leaving office. Allegations of corruption are now looming over the administration of Rod Blagojevich.

Perry Cobb got a job as a janitor in a Chicago apartment building but he gave up his old singing career. His experience on death row had broken his confidence. Darby Tillis became a preacher and tries to help released death-row prisoners adjust to life outside. He said that prisoners try to take their sentence like a man. But then they get to death row, where they are hit by the stench: disinfectant, faeces, urine, body odour, sick odour. 'You sit there and await death, and the pain you know will come to you some day.'

*I enjoyed your letter as always in spite of you not having no news! You said that the doctor advised against drinking with the new medication you are on. It's an honor that you are willing to accept the drink ban willingly as a sign of solidarity with me in my situation. I got the postcard you sent of the African art work – that is something, huh?*

*The new basketball shoes are great! No more playing with cardboard in my shoe – you found that funny since you could relate to having your mother put paper in your shoes to keep out the wet. You know sometimes you have to do what you have to do to get by until you can see a better day. My better day came with the new shoes and I've not missed a day of basketball yet, I felt like a new man the first day I went out there and jumped up in the air. I wish you could see me play one day, I would be honored to show you some of my moves, bouncing the ball between my legs, behind my back, then spinning around the defender before shootin' a jump shot!*

*Since my last letter a couple of things have changed in my life. One – Dan, my best friend – has moved, he had his case overturned to escape the death sentence, he's now carrying the sentence of life without parole. This is bitter-sweet for me as well as him. We'd grew very close over the years. He got his sentence overturned because his crime was committed while he was a juvenile. He lived next door to me, now he's in population [the ordinary prison population], where I wish to be one day. This was and will be a difficult transition for me, however I must continue to move on, it's a must. My new neighbor, he's quiet right now. He hasn't got comfortable yet. It usually takes two months, then their personalities start to show. I've spoken to him, he seems like an okay guy. I doubt if he'll become as good a friend as Dan was. I'll keep you posted. Two – I'm a hall runner, which means I come out of my cell, pretty much a trustee, I'm allowed out of my cell three days a week to assist the other inmates with hot water for coffee or tea, heat their food in the microwave, pass out their trays, do things they can't do from their cell. I was a hall runner before but I got into trouble and got fired, you could say.*

Justice Antonin Scalia of the US Supreme Court believes that the Constitution is not a 'living' document to be interpreted by successive generations, as the Old and New Testaments have been and are still being variously interpreted. Justice Scalia argues that those who framed the Constitution did not restrict the death penalty and so the Supreme Court erred when in 1988 it outlawed the execution of offenders who had committed their crimes while under the age of sixteen.

However, the following year, the Supreme Court ruled that sixteen- to eighteen-year-olds could be killed by the government – despite the fact that American youths under age eighteen are legally prohibited from witnessing executions, as well as joining the military and fighting in battle, voting, purchasing alcohol or tobacco, or signing legal contracts.

The reason given for excluding juveniles from such activities is their lack of maturity, which is why most countries adhere to the worldwide standard of protecting minors from execution. While adolescents should be held accountable for their actions, scientific information shows that they cannot be held accountable to the same extent as adults. Studies by the Harvard Medical School and the National Institute of Mental Health found that the parts of the brain which regulate impulse control and judgement are not fully developed in adolescents. Development is not completed until somewhere between eighteen and twenty-two years of age. These findings confirm that adolescents generally are more impulsive: they are more likely to make unsound judgments and are less aware of the consequences of their actions. Juveniles are also more likely to be coerced and used by more experienced criminals. They are often intimidated by authority figures and forced to make false confessions. More importantly, the aims of the death penalty do not apply to juveniles. The retribution of the death penalty aims to give the harshest punishment to the worst offender – juveniles are the most likely to be capable of rehabilitation. The state's duty should be to help them do this rather than kill them.

The US led the world in the execution of juveniles and it was completely out of line with the human-rights practices of most other countries. In refusing to ratify the UN Convention on the Rights of the Child, the US gave as its main objection that it would be required to abandon the killing of juvenile offenders. Juvenile executions are still allowed in the Congo, Iran, Nigeria, Pakistan, Saudi Arabia, China, Yemen and DR Congo – not great company for democratic USA.

Approximately 365 persons have been executed in the US for juvenile crimes since 1608, that is, 1.8 percent of roughly 20,000 confirmed American executions since that time. Twenty-two of these executions for juvenile crimes have been imposed since the reinstatement of the death penalty in 1976, thirteen of them in Texas. These twenty-two executions make up about 2 percent of the total executions since 1976.

Worldwide, there were fifteen executions of juveniles in the period 1997 to 2001; the US killed nine of the fifteen. Between 1990 and September 2004, thirty-eight juveniles around the world were executed; nineteen of them were executed in the US. By mid-2003, there were seventy-eight juveniles on death row in thirteen states, twenty-eight of them in Texas.

Gradually, public opinion in the US has begun to oppose the execution of juvenile offenders. According to a 2003 Harris Poll, 69 percent of the people polled opposed the death penalty for juveniles; only 22 percent supported the execution of juvenile offenders, while 9 percent offered no opinion. Meanwhile, the juvenile death penalty disproportionately affected children of colour and showed the same racial disparities as were evident throughout the use of capital punishment.

On 27 January 2004, the US Supreme Court decided to review whether executing sixteen- and seventeen-year-olds violates the Constitution's ban on cruel and unusual punishment. The review came after the Missouri Supreme Court overturned the death sentence of seventeen-year-old Christopher Simmons. Four of the judges called the juvenile death penalty 'inconsistent with evolving standards of decency in a civilized society'.

Almost a year later, a sharply divided Supreme Court ruled on 1 March 2005 that the death penalty cannot be imposed on murderers who were not yet eighteen years of age at the time they committed the crimes, thus ending a practice used in nineteen US states. Such executions are a disproportionate punishment for juveniles, whom society views as categorically less culpable than adult criminals, the Court said, and violate the ban on cruel and unusual punishment contained in the Eighth Amendment to the US Constitution. It is thought that the Court may have been influenced by a desire to end the United States' international isolation on the issue. The five-to-four decision threw out the current death sentences of seventy-two juvenile murderers and barred states from seeking to execute minors in the future.

Justice Anthony Kennedy, giving the majority opinion, said 'Neither retribution nor deterrence provides adequate justification for imposing the death penalty on juvenile offenders.' Justices John Paul Stevens, David H. Souter, Ruth Bader Ginsberg and Stephen Breyer joined Justice Kennedy in the decision.

In a dissent that highlighted the federal-versus-states' rights aspects of the Constitution, Justice Antonin Scalia strongly criticised his colleagues for taking power from the states. Chief Justice William Rehnquist and Justices Sandra Day O'Connor and Clarence Thomas joined Justice Scalia in his dissent.

By far the greatest impact of the Supreme Court ruling was felt in Texas, where there were twenty-nine juvenile offenders awaiting execution, and in Alabama, where there were fourteen. No other state had more than five juveniles on death row.

* * *

A closer look at one of the states just mentioned, Alabama, is not encouraging. It may seem unfair to pick out one state, but it is necessary so that readers may learn more about how the death-penalty system works in a state that seems enthusiastic about the implementation of the system.

There are approximately two hundred people currently sentenced to death in Alabama. In recent years, Alabama has sentenced more people to death per capita than any other state in the US. In 2005, Alabama sentenced more people to death than the neighbouring states of Georgia, Mississippi, Louisiana and Tennessee combined. At a time when the number of death sentences nationwide is steadily declining, the number of people sentenced to death in Alabama in 2006 increased by 16.6 percent. With a population of only 4.5 million people, Alabama's total of thirteen new death sentences in 2007 was higher than the eleven new death sentences imposed in Texas, which has a population of 23.5 million people. What would people in Ireland – which has roughly the same population as Alabama – think if thirteen people were sentenced to death here every year?

Alabama is now the only state in the US that permits judges to override jury verdicts of life without parole and impose death sentences instead. Approximately 22 percent of Alabama's death-row prisoners received life verdicts that were later overridden – in favour of the death penalty – by elected trial judges. In 2006, an election year, the number of death sentences imposed by judges overriding jury verdicts increased to 28 percent.

Almost all of Alabama's elected judges campaign on their strong support for the death penalty, and some may even promise to facilitate executions in order to get votes. Alabama is well known for high spending on judicial campaigns. Since 1993, candidates competing for seats on Alabama's Supreme Court spent over $54 million on their campaigns – far exceeding judicial campaign spending in any other state. In 2006, one candidate for chief justice spent $7.7 million, taking second place in the list of most costly judicial campaigns in US history.

One Alabama Supreme Court judge pledged to resist compliance with the US Supreme Court's 2005 ban on executing juveniles and has referred to the Court's invocation of international law on this issue as 'ridiculous' and 'judicial tryranny'.

Over half of Alabama's death-row prisoners were represented by attorneys appointed at trial, who, under state law, could only be paid $1,000 for the time they spent preparing the case for trial. There are nearly a dozen death-row prisoners who have no legal representation. Many death-row prisoners were represented by attorneys who have subsequently been disbarred, suspended or disciplined for misconduct. In some cases, lawyers were found to have been intoxicated or impaired during the trial.

Despite the fact that each year 65 percent of all homicide victims in Alabama are black, nearly 80 percent of the people on Alabama's death row have been condemned for crimes involving victims who are white. In over twenty death-penalty cases, courts have found that Alabama prosecutors have illegally excluded African-Americans from jury service through racially discriminatory jury-selection procedures.

Nearly half of Alabama's death row is black, even though blacks make up just 27 percent of the total population of the state. Over 60 percent of those executed in the state since 1976 have been African-American.

In the US, since 1976, there have been 129 exonerations of innocent death-row prisoners: for every eight people executed, one innocent person has been exonerated. Seven people have been exonerated in Alabama.

Federal courts refused to stay three executions in Alabama during the spring and summer of 2007 despite numerous requests to review lethal-injection procedures due to serious concerns that lethal injection is torturous to condemned prisoners. It was not until 25 September 2007 that the US Supreme Court agreed to address whether lethal-injection methods violate the Eighth Amendment's 'cruel and unusual punishment' clause. Since then, the Supreme Court has stayed executions around the country. Forty-two people who contested the lethal-injection method were executed earlier in 2007 in the United States.

# 8

## Prison Life

No serious news, Ray, just trivial stuff. Tomás fixed the DVD machine last week – it was very difficult, there was one lead loose! Too much for me! So to celebrate, we got *Walk the Line* – we had being minding Cathal for 37 hours, 16 minutes and 4 seconds while his mom and dad were at a wedding in Belfast – so all was quiet again and, with the house restored to its usual condition, we relaxed with the film. We enjoyed it very much, the story was true and the songs were good.

I liked when the prison governor asked Johnny Cash not to sing songs which reminded prisoners of where they were and Johnny said: 'Do you think they've forgotten?' The actor looked amazingly like Johnny Cash himself. I don't know what to think of prison scenes where everybody is singing along and everything seems fine, no problems, etc . . . can prison life be like that? I thought Johnny recovered from his addiction a bit too quick? I'm sure it was more of a struggle than the film showed. I remember a film I saw years ago – *The Man with the Golden Arm* with Jack Lemmon (I think) and Kim Novak (I'm sure!) – I think that really showed the struggle with addiction.

No real news here, just plodding along day by day – it's good to be able to say that. You remember the people in Mayo who don't want Shell to lay gas pipes through their land and build a refinery on land? Some of them walked in the last two weeks from Mayo to Dublin to meet people in the towns and to let people know why they were protesting. They are getting very little coverage in the newspapers. The walk was about 250 miles. I asked one of them did they put any special cream on their feet. 'Not at all. Good runners, and soak the feet in warm water at night, is all you need!' I thought of you. May you play lots of good basketball in the new runners.

I was very surprised that you know of Brendan Behan (1923–1964), he was a famous Dublin character. He was alive when I first came to Dublin but I never saw him. The house I stayed in at that time was just a couple of streets away from the house where he was born. His grandmother used bring him to funerals, and after the funerals it was the custom to go to the pub. His grandmother started giving Brendan sips of Guinness stout and he himself said that he thought he must have been an alcoholic by the age of ten or eleven. He drank lots of 'mountain dew' – not your US soda! I read his book of jail writings, *The Borstal Boy*, years ago – at that time this book and lots of others which gave a bad/true picture of Ireland were banned here, could not be sold, but people could always get them from England or Belfast, which is in that part of Ireland still ruled by the British. Now you can buy any kind of book here. One song he wrote became famous and is still sung in pubs. 'Tis called 'The Auld Triangle' and is set in your misnamed prison, Mountjoy. The triangle was hit to announce mealtimes and so on. They have it in a glass case in Mountjoy now.

> A hungry feeling came o'er me stealing,
> And the mice they were squealing in my prison cell.
> And the auld triangle went jingle jangle
> All along the banks of the Royal Canal.

* * *

*I found it funny you said you made the mistake of passing Cathal in through the kitchen window and now he wants to go through it every time he's out in the garden. And, yes, I do think it's a bit late to say 'before he rules our lives'! I think it's good for the both of you, him and y'all. He'll keep y'all minds sharp and alert and he's gathering lots of memories of his grandparents.*

*You're right. We certainly don't have the same taste in music! I like rap, hip-hop music like Tupac Shakur and Jay-Z. I'm sure you're not familiar with them two artists. I also like slow music, mood-setting music, lovemaking music. I'm just like you, I can't sing a note either. Yes, I've heard a crow, we both sound like that. You said when your dancing partner at Catherine's wedding said you had rhythm, that was one of the best compliments you've ever gotten. I would like to see what the girl saw and be the judge of that!*

Your poem, Ray – 'Calling All Bets' – has great rhythm, a great natural kind of run to it. I could write an article for a paper but I don't even know how to begin to write a poem like that.

Thanks for asking abour Rahim and Hamid. They are both well. I think they are very lonely for home. I think the two of them would understand better than most how you must feel. . . . Rahim has no bad effects at all from the hunger strike and I don't think any charges will be brought against them. The authorities would probably prefer to let it all die down. The hunger strike may not have been too wise but still I felt I should support Rahim on a personal level. That was not very difficult. Afghans in Norway are also threatening hunger strike.

Róisín had to get glasses before they go to Chicago to visit her US granny. The frames, of course, had to be in her favourite colour – pink. All the young girls of her age here are mad about pink – clothes, shoes, school bags, bicycles, everything. Is Rachel pink-mad or is green her colour?

Róisín's mom, I'm afraid, had a 'bruising' journey to Chicago – the man in the seat beside her weighed 350 pounds! He was very nice and they had a grand chat but she had no room nor did she get any sleep, even though he would have been a nice soft pillow!

By all accounts they are enjoying themselves in the US. Eoin is doing lots of sports and Róisín did a short course for kids on how to cross the street and general road safety – she definitely needs some lessons in that. She said the best part of the course was when a policeman came to talk to them and 'he had a gun in a holster'!

How are the headaches these days? Rahim gets headaches also. Could it be from the tension in your situations? He was here with Hamid one day last week. We cut the very overgrown front hedge; well, Rahim did most of the work while Hamid cooked an Afghan dinner for us. It was a change from hostel food for them, and we enjoyed it too. Hamid is not very strong really and you'd be a bit worried about him.

I'm glad your new neighbour seems okay. The way you described it brought home to me what a shock it must be to find yourself on death row. We were at a play about the death penalty during the week – one of the characters said: 'It's hard to write poetry in here' – I thought of you – and then he said: 'but I sing'. The play, *The Exonerated*, had ten characters sitting in a row across the stage and each of them played a few parts – I think I'd read about most of what they said but it was kind of chilling to hear somebody else say the words. The play has been going around the world for the past five or six years and they get 'celebrity' actors to play one or more parts. We got David Soul, who used to be the fair-haired cop in *Starsky and Hutch* on TV. All the actors were in the bar afterwards. We got David Soul's autograph! He seems a nice guy but looks a bit older than when he was Starsky. Or was he Hutch?

* * *

*The book you spoke of reading by Sister Helen Prejean, I've heard of her before, she's very involved in getting this death penalty abolished. You said after reading it, you wanted to go for a long walk. I bet you did. It makes you appreciate freedom and being able to go for a walk, don't it?*

*An inmate now is lucky to see fifteen years, some of the laws were changed and that speeded up the process. We had an execution this week, the guy had been here about sixteen years. He wanted to die, I'd talked to him before but didn't know him very well. He seemed like a good dude, he'd just given up. He was saying if he couldn't get back out there to his family, he'd rather die, and he was at peace with dyin'. Lord forbid I ever get that type of mentality. This place does drain one's hopes and it erases dreams. It's physically and mentally testing. I've been here for a number of executions and usually the victim, as I'll call those inmates who's passed away, come to accept that they're taking their last walk. I've yet to see one refuse to walk and get taken to the execution chamber by force. I've always said, and I still have the mentality, that I want to be able to go that easy if I have to take the last walk but I really don't think I'll be able to do it. I've had this discussion with a number of guys here that's been here over twenty years and they told me that a lot of guys have the same mentality but as time passed, they become more accepting of their fate and go in peace. One guy here is fifty-five years old, he's been on death row twenty-three years and had a stay in the death cell once. He told me that once he went to the cell for two days with a head full of black hair, after his trip it all was grey, his entire head of hair is white grey.*

*Yes, it was very inspiring when I was found guilty of this crime, to have the victim's family not pursue the death penalty. . . . So I'm able to keep my spirits up by feeding off the love, support and compassion of those that's there for me when I need them, like my family, Michael, all of you. I know I'll be letting you down if I let this place get the best of me and I use that to press forward and keep my spirits up. So I do it for more than myself, do that make sense? Well, my friend, I'll end there. Take care.*

An increasing number of families of victims are deciding not to look for vengeance and instead are finding the courage to search for peace and reconciliation. Who can even begin to understand the pain and suffering that the families of murder victims must feel; the pain that lasts all day every day, an incurable wound? Or the pain of the mother of a person who is executed, who often sees her family being treated like vermin and subjected to all kinds of horrible abuse?

Members of murder victims' support groups such as Survive and Murder Victims' Families for Human Rights are helping each other face their great losses without demanding the death of the perpetrators. Many politicians say they want restricted use of the death penalty: they want to reserve it for crimes which are 'the worst of the worst'. But these crimes are impossible to determine, according to anti-death penalty campaigners. Many politicians also say that the families of victims deserve to see justice done and that executions bring closure for families.

As part of his campaign to become governor of New York state in 1994, George Pataki claimed that the death penalty should be restored as a deterrent. Following his election, New York once again had the death penalty on its statute books, but the implementation of the law was very costly. Hundreds of capital murder cases were processed and by 2004 a grand total of five people had been sent to death row – at a cost of $170 million to the taxpayer. Since then, the New York Supreme Court found the statute to be unconstitutional. That vast sum of money could have been well spent in two ways: one, on real anti-crime measures, helping at-risk youths, setting up drug rehabilitation clinics for indigent youths; and two, on providing adequate funding for victim-support groups, for medical care and counselling, and for compensation for things like lost wages.

The abolition of the death penalty in New Jersey at the end of 2007 was the culmination of an eight-year campaign by Larry Post, the father of a murder victim, who came to the conclusion that capital punishment served no useful purpose. Post founded New Jerseyans for Alternatives to the Death Penalty. Started in a church basement, the group grew to 12,000 members and forged an unusual coalition of clerics, members of both political parties, families of murder victims and law-enforcement officials, all of whom decided that they wanted a change. A statewide poll taken earlier in 2007 showed that, by a margin of 51 percent to 41 percent, the people of New Jersey preferred that criminals be sentenced to life in prison without parole instead of being sentenced to death. In late November 2007, family members of sixty-two murder victims sent a letter to legislators urging passage of the abolition Bill. The relatives emphasised the personal toll the process had taken on them. 'Capital punishment drags victims' loved ones through an agonising and lengthy process, holding out the promise of one punishment in the beginning and often resulting in a life sentence in the end anyway', the relatives said in a statement.

On 4 January 2008, the *Kansas City Star* published this letter from Renny Cushing, executive director of Murder Victims' Families for Human Rights: 'New Jersey legislators recently voted to abolish the death penalty and New Jersey's governor signed the legislation. As someone who has suffered the loss of losing a loved one to murder, I salute the state for its actions.

'When my father was murdered, my family and I did not feel that an execution would give us peace. We did not believe that another killing would honor our father's memory or the values he instilled in us. Since that time, I have met and worked closely with hundreds of other murder victims' family members who agree that responding to one killing with another killing doesn't help anyone.

'The death penalty offers a false promise of closure to victims' families, who are led to believe that an execution will bring relief. While families wait through the lengthy, roller-coaster appeals process, reliving our original pain again and again, the focus remains on the murderer rather than on the victims or on our own anguish as surviving family members. The death penalty is a distraction from victims' real needs, not a solution.'

We were really sorry to hear about the execution. It must be traumatic for you all. Imagine being so down that dying didn't bother him, or at least that he was ready to die. You are great, Ray, the way you keep your spirits up. You work at it so positively. We are always happy to listen to what you say.

There have been about 130 'volunteer' executions – almost 12 percent of the more than 1,100 executions since the death penalty was reinstated in 1976. The 'volunteers' are the prisoners who forego all their rights to appeal and who no longer wish to overturn their death sentence. 'State-assisted suicide' or 'prisoner-assisted homicide' are the phrases used. There are a number of reasons why a prisoner may drop his appeal: mental or physical illness, remorse, confinement and loneliness (and in some prisons the lack of any contact visits), the fact that life without parole seems frightening and unbearable, despair about the prospect of appealing successfully, or a wish to exert some control over a situation in which one is, in fact, totally powerless.

The State of Mississippi executed Bobby Glen Wilcher (44, white) on 18 October 2006, for stabbing two women to death. He was nineteen at the time of his crime. He had been on death row for more than twenty years.

Wilcher said that he would not make any further appeals. His lawyers argued that he should have a mental assessment to determine whether he was competent – because of his bipolar disorder and a history of psychological problems – to make such a decision. The court found Wilcher competent to waive his appeal at a hearing convened at short notice and without any expert witnesses being called.

Three years earlier, in May 2003, Judge Jerry Davis ruled that conditions in the Mississippi state prison offended 'contemporary concepts of decency, human dignity and precepts of civilisation which we profess to possess'. He was ruling in a lawsuit filed by the American Civil Liberties Union (ACLU) on behalf of six prisoners who alleged that harsh conditions were contributing to a high rate of mental illness among inmates. It is thought that this was the first successful death-row-conditions case in the United States. In 2003, there were sixty-six men and one woman on death row in Mississippi.

In his ruling, Davis found that the way inmates were treated constituted cruel and unusual punishment, in violation of the Eighth Amendment. He said: 'No one in a civilised society should be forced to live under conditions that force exposure to another person's body waste. No matter how heinous the crimes committed, there is no excuse for such living conditions.' Davis found that death-row inmates were being subjected to 'profound isolation, intolerable stench and filth, consistent exposure to human excrement, dangerously high temperatures and humidity, insect infestations, deprivation of basic mental health care, constant exposure to severely psychotic inmates'.

The judge instructed the Mississippi Corrections Department to undertake a number of reforms, including annual mental-health check-ups, upgraded lighting and toilet plumbing, provision of cleaning materials, and all windows to be repaired and fitted with screens to protect the prisoners from insects.

Prisoners had complained about the stifling heat and lack of ventilation. Davis said that if the heat exceeded ninety degrees, each cell should be fitted with a fan and ice water, and showers should also be available. The prison authorities should also provide sneakers and a shaded area for exercise, with access to water. At that time, prisoners wore prison-issue flip-flops in individual exercise cages.

Corrections commissioner Chris Epps said that he did not consider Mississippi's death row any worse than others across the country and he 'respectfully' disagreed with the judge's findings. He shrugged off suggestions that something had to be done about sweltering prison cells. 'It's hot in the Delta,' he said.

Margaret Winter of the ACLU believed that the ruling set a precedent for standards on death row. It recognised the basic principle in our society that 'we treat everybody humanely, we don't subject anybody to torture'. The lawsuit may have forced the authorities to improve the conditions for prisoners but the struggle to ensure adequate medical and mental health care for prisoners is an ongoing one. Five summers after the Mississippi case, Ray and his fellow prisoners still swelter in their narrow cells. Surely the fact that such conditions can exist in the twenty-first century is a shame and a disgrace. As this is being written, the radio news tells of overcrowding, poor physical conditions and the continuing use of slopping out in Irish prisons.

Carolyn Clayton, who helped found the victims'-rights group Survive Inc., said that she could not disagree with the Davis ruling. 'Even though they've done some horrific things, they are still human beings,' she said.

*You said you were glad to come back from your visit to your sister in Cork when you did! I bet you were, finding the toilet overflowing on you! Now that's something I've had to deal with here far more often than I would care to think about. Last month we had overflows at least twice. They would come to fix them, run a long kind of implement through the pipes, and it would work for an hour, and then it's back overflowing. My cell and four others are on the same line, so if any one of them got something flushed that shouldn't be, it causes all five to back up. So I can relate to the toilet overflow you speak of even though it's not funny at all when it's happening. About that book you like,* Toilets of the World, *is it actually about toilets? Some book! I'm not sure I would find stories of toilets interesting but I would give it a try if you'd like me to read it!!*

* * *

*I have your letter here with me which I'll answer in a second. I just feel like talking right now, sharing my thoughts. You told me never to hesitate. Correct? Do you know I've never thought about killing myself in all of my twenty-seven years? And I've experienced some pretty hard times and saw enough death and struggle to drive a man crazy. I think all that I encountered growing up built me to endure these tough times. I grew up around violence, I used to wake up to my father beating my mother, if not woken by him or by one of my drunken uncles wanting to wrestle. I would rather be woken up to wrestle than have him jumping on my mother. Nights like these never fade out of your memories, it be the good times that fade. I remember how I used to get up when I heard them first start to argue and go in my sister's room before they start to fight. One particular night, I was fourteen years old and I came home from my aunt's house to find my mother's lip burst with stitches in it, it made her so unattractive. Soon as I saw her I asked what happened and she told me she fell at work. Always it's she fell, even when I've heard it the night before.*

*When I turned fifteen years old I was bigger and stronger than my dad. When we wrestled, I always handled him with ease. We once broke a table in my mother's living room, I slammed him on it. My mother was so upset when it broke, she woke up yelling and pushing both of us out of the living room. My father was upset I threw him down like I did, he wanted to go outside in the yard, it was the early hours of the morning, he was really drunk, I wanted to go outside too. I went and put my shoes on, we went outside and I slammed him again. After that I was never afraid of him again.*

*I remember telling my sisters don't be scared of him, he ain't big enough, he knew it. When I'd hear him raising his voice or arguing with my mother, I'd get up and go downstairs or knock on their bedroom door to let them know I'm woke up. . . . I love and loved my dad, believe it or not, I just didn't like him jumping on my mother. He never hit my sisters, never.*

*He wasn't the best father but he taught me a lot about the streets and how to live in them. He went away to prison for a year and while he was away, my mother got her life back together, she stopped using and started going to nursing school. I was too far in the streets to get out of them. Gang banging, dealing drugs, just living how I saw normal. But as I've had the time to sit here, incarcerated, I think back and I was truly living reckless.*

*When my father got out, I was about to turn seventeen, with a car and my own apartment with my girlfriend. He got out and got back on crack cocaine. My mother wouldn't have him back unless he got help. He stopped but not for long and to this very day he's still an addict out there smoking crack. As I got older I noticed the way the family treated him, they lost all trust, he stole from them so much they didn't allow him in their houses at one time, unless they needed him to do something. I didn't like that. He'd stolen from me but that's my father. I knew he was an addict and I'd grew up around them. Right before I turned eighteen my father went to prison again and when he was getting out, I was incarcerated getting ready to go on trial. . .*

*Why I told you all that, I don't know. Just had it on my mind, letting you into my life. . . . Well, I'll get to your letter now. . . .*

* * *

*Your letters were like fresh breaths. . . . I'm sorry to put a damper on your day with my news of the court denying my appeal. I was disappointed and angry with that news, it wasn't expected. And it's even more frustrating when you know there's good relevant issues and grounds that'll get me off death row and the courts won't even pay attention to them. As you stated, it's like the people that has the power to do the right thing are reluctant to do that in fear of the backlash. It's sad.*

*I must admit this process of dealing with the situation is really wearing on me but what can I do about it? This is what it's designed for, to hammer away at my sanity and make me feel worthless and give up hope. I refuse to let them win. I feel I've come too far to turn back now or let them win, you feel me?*

*I was talking to this guy here about two weeks ago. He's not on death row, he's sixty years old, been in prison since 1970 and has a sentence of a hundred years. He was put in a cell here for trying to escape. When I was talking to him I thought to myself I would take those hundred years any day over this sentence I have now. And that was so very painful to realise. For me to see one hundred years in prison as freedom, to be content with that, that is painful. Not in a million years would I have thought I'd end up here. Not only do the prison rules make it harder but the repeated cycle of every day, stuck in an 8' x 5' cell with barely enough room to spread my arms. Do you know if I spread my arms I could touch each side of the wall with the palms of my hands. I'm basically stuck inside a clothes closet twenty-three hours a day, this isn't something I would wish on anyone. It's not wise to constantly dwell on this life here.*

9

# One-year Anniversary

No real news here except for our short trip to Rossport in Mayo to protest at Shell's attempts to build an on-shore gas refinery. The previous week the Guards had been very tough on the protestors, who have made official complaints about the behaviour of the Guards. The area is beautiful for miles and miles. Beautiful sea views and huge cliffs. The local people fear that the refinery will spoil the area and also that the emissions from the refinery will spoil the wildlife in the sea. There's also the danger of explosions in the gas pipeline.

We stayed in a hostel on the Sunday night and a man from the area whom we know came over with his wife. They are under fierce pressure because of the protests and trying to keep on a job at the same time. So what would we have for supper? We couldn't just have a cup of tea by itself – so once again Bríd to the rescue, who in the wilds of Mayo produced this box which had a fruit cake inside it! A miracle! We were going to bring the cake down to Catherine and Martin the next day but we ate half of it before the blazing fire.

The next morning we got up about 6 AM and headed off down the road towards the gates of the proposed gas refinery, where about a hundred people were gathering, cold, huddled together. It was still dark. Am I making it dramatic enough? The best is yet to come! About 7.30 two vanloads of Guards appeared and stood around. Another vanload was in the background. Then along the road we saw the lights of a huge fleet of lorries and trucks bringing workers in to start building the refinery. Our job was to stop them but the Guards, with linked arms, had us hemmed in. It was eyeball-to-eyeball stuff. Couldn't get a smile at all from any Guard. Were they big and strong!

The boss Guard shouted: 'Hold the line' and all the protestors laughed and shouted back: 'Hold the line'! Then somebody found a gap and suddenly we had a 'sit down' in the middle of the road by about twenty young people. The Guards filmed them and then went around afterwards and asked them their names and addresses quite aggressively. I thought that they were definitely trying to intimidate them but the young people knew their rights, gave the Guards the minimum information and insisted on seeing their ID cards.

Then the Guards that were in reserve marched up the road under the command of the sergeant, who seemingly trained as a riot-squad commander. A local fellow I knew sat down on the road and I sat behind him. Bríd was kind of nervous at this stage! I don't know whether they filmed me or not but they never looked for my name or anything afterwards.

The super cop came along, tapped me on the shoulder and said: 'Remove this gentleman!' Shows what a bad judge of character he was to call me a 'gentleman'! So two huge Guards carried me to the side of the road and dropped me, where I was welcomed by Bríd. Other days they just threw protestors into the ditch – including a member of parliament one day.

Then the super cop announced that he was closing the road to pedestrians and we were all hemmed into the side of the road. I was shocked when I heard Bríd questioning the Guards. It must be the company she keeps! The protest was over about 9 AM – the workers had got into the site and everybody stood around talking. I said to one older Guard: 'You're taking my photo, can I take yours?' 'Sure,' he said, and kind of lowered the camera and kind of smiled!

There was an independent filmmaker there who asked me would I say a few words. So I said my few fiery words and the people standing around applauded! At one stage I said to myself 'What would Ray think?' and I imagined you throwing your eyes to heaven and saying: 'That old couple shouldn't be let out! After all my talk and warnings to them to take care! I might as well have kept my mouth shut!'

*I am doing okay today, basically just trucking along and keeping my faith. I can't allow myself to stay down in the dumps too long. I think life is too short for that and will only lessen my chances of picking myself back up and fighting the next battle. I must save something for the next fight if it don't turn out as planned, so I'll be able to carry on to the next, you feel me? I'm not a quitter, I've never been and never will be. Sooner or later my time will come, and when it do, all my disappointing stages and moments will be worth the wait.*

*This day last year was a great day for me, it was the day you decided to find out more about me. We've developed a nice relationship and I've gathered an Irish family. I couldn't ask for more than that. Well, maybe freedom. Thanks for everything, I'll always cherish the support, concern and bond we've developed over this year.*

*All that needs to be said is in the poem. Words really don't do the gratefulness justice, but you're intelligent, I'm sure you'll get it!!*

*This poem is just a thank you*
*for all the kindness shown*
*for letting me know the pain I felt*
*is gone.*

*It's all your caring letters*
*that you wrote to show you're there*
*it's for making my load lighter*
*and easier for me to bear.*

*It's for the many, many smiles*
*you've brought to my face*
*for letting me feel your concern and support*
*while inside this ugly, hateful place.*

*It's for listening to my problems*
*and the things that bother me*
*it's for every single time*
*you've filled my heart with glee.*

*It's for every time I've written*
*and you've written me back again*
*it's for showing me there is*
*a 100 percent true friend – in deed.*

*I feel deep in my heart that I'm blessed to have such friends as you all. You make it evident that you appreciate me as a person. You make me feel human. I hope this letter of mine finds you and the family doing fine, taking care. It's 10* PM. *I've had some noodle soup and crackers and now I'm sitting here drinking me a soda. I would write more but I'm beat right now. Slán.*

Many thanks for your poem, Ray. We had a really good laugh at you saying you were nervous just reading my account of the Guards lifting us off the road and saying old couples like us shouldn't be let out and that yes, you should have kept your mouth shut if we were going to ignore your 'take good care' advice. Ray, you are 110 percent right!

The funny thing is that I was nervous the night before and I was nervous that morning but once the action started I wasn't a bit nervous. And the people from the area were so nice, making sure we were all right.

* * *

*Any time when I speak about things such as people being executed, it's not easy but I know those type of things need to be let out and not held in and I wanted to let you know some of my thoughts on that, I know I don't speak of that type of stuff often. I believe that bravery comes from strengthening yourself in every way and getting yourself into a particular mindset to face challenges. To an onlooker that can look as if it comes natural but it doesn't by no means. I would like to think, in any situation, I'll be brave and able to handle it. But I certainly don't want to have to find out if I'm able to 'man up' on this. 'Man up' is a phrase we use, pretty much saying 'be brave'. I do agree that it's a great tribute to the people with me that I've never seen a man who didn't walk for his last time. . . .*

The death-penalty system is a cruel system. On 4 February 2008, the *Birmingham News* reported on the unnecessary cruelty suffered by two families because of the eagerness of state prosecutors to proceed with an execution.

The normal path to a killer's execution is immensely traumatic for two families – the killer's family, and the family of his victims. There are trials, there are appeals, execution dates are set, followed by delays. At every step along the journey, hopes are raised on one side, dashed on the other. So it was in the case of James Harvey

Callahan, who was sentenced to death for kidnapping, raping and killing a Jacksonville State University student in 1982. An execution date was set and then stayed.

But what happened in Callahan's case proved that an overzealous prosecutor can take a bad situation and make it worse. To be sure, the victim's family most likely would have liked to see Callahan's execution go through as scheduled. But in December 2007, US District Judge Keith Watkins postponed the execution with good reasons: he wanted first to hear Callahan's challenge to Alabama's lethal-injection procedures, and he also said he would not schedule that hearing until the US Supreme Court heard a similar challenge from Kentucky. It would be a 'waste of judicial resources' to do so. Watkins' ruling came soon after the US Supreme Court blocked the execution of another Alabama inmate – this was one of a series of decisions that led in September 2007 to the Supreme Court placing a moratorium on executions until it had ruled on the lethal-injection issue.

But instead of waiting for that decision, Alabama's Attorney-General, Troy King, appealed the Callahan stay to the 11th US Circuit Court of Appeals. The 11th Circuit ruled that Callahan had not raised his challenge to Alabama's lethal-injection procedures in a timely way, and lifted the stay. By the time the US Supreme Court intervened to block the execution, Callahan was a little more than an hour away from being put to death. He had visited with his family to say his goodbyes and the prison system had gone through the necessary motions to prepare for the execution.

Even worse, the mother and sister of his victim had already travelled to Alabama to witness the execution. The family called the ordeal 'cruel and unusual'. The *Birmingham News* said: 'They are right, and King should be ashamed. King is eager to carry out executions. Tough on crime and all that. Everyone gets it. But to appeal Callahan's stay before the Supreme Court had ruled on the lethal-injection case was to waste prison officials' time and to give two families an extra twist through a wringer that's painful enough. It was cruel, and unnecessary.'

* * *

Christmas here is like Thanksgiving in the US, I think, with turkey as the main dish. Now to the plum pudding you asked about. You take raisins, sultanas, other dried fruit, flour, Guinness, breadcrumbs, eggs, spice and more Guinness, and you mix it all together and leave it in a big bowl on the table. Everybody who comes into the house gives the mixture a stir. People say that they stir their wishes into the mixture but that is really just a way to make sure the mixture is well stirred!

Then you cook or steam that for hours and hours in a bowl which gives the pudding its shape. At Christmas you put a sprig of holly on top of it, pour whiskey over it and set the whiskey on fire.

One time you would start making the pudding for the following Christmas a month or so after Christmas was over. The idea was to let the pudding mature, as it improves with age, so they say. Nowadays I'd say many people buy Christmas puddings in the shop just before Christmas but the old tradition survives in many houses too. And as my mother used to say: 'You always recognise the real thing.'

Rahim and Hamid were here yesterday and were talking about a custom they have. They cook this huge dish of food mostly made from wheat. It must be cooked over a fire for two to three days, so family, relations and friends take turns sitting around the huge bowl, stirring all the time, night and day. Sometimes it's an excuse for some drinking and also for some singing. Sounds a bit more exciting than our Christmas-pudding making!

*Another Christmas on top of us! No, Christmas doesn't really excite me any more, it's just become another day for me, pretty much like all the other holidays, so many of them pass and it's no different than the regular days of every month. I just be grateful to be around and to be here for another*

*Christmas. I did get the incentive box – and the food in it – that the prison allows us get at this time of year. I've been enjoying the different foods, the sweet candy, Skittles, Starburst. Have you heard of those candies? They're like different chewy candies with different flavors throughout the package. I've been really enjoying the box of food and thanks for the funds to buy the things I wanted. I enjoyed being able to eat something different. I eat lots of cereal throughout the day and the night if I have the milk. Are you familiar with cereal?*

*No, I didn't get a visit this Christmas either. I was supposed to get one in December but the radiator in my mother's car sprung a leak and she didn't, or couldn't, get it fixed so she cancelled and now, with her having had already took that day off from work, she must wait thirty days to get another day off. And one of my lil sisters got a new job, like late November, so she can't just take off from work, not having been working there long.*

*I was able to talk to them on Christmas Eve, collect call. My mother had Rachel at her house with my nieces and nephew while my lil sisters went out to a local club. She was cooking and trying to make them behave at the same time. I found it funny to hear them laughing and enjoying themselves. . . . The girls didn't want my nephew in the room with them, he had gas and was letting it go in their presence! My nephew, being the only boy, is going to go through some things with those girls. I too had to go through that.*

*Anyway, as I was about to say, I asked all of them what they wanted to get tomorrow on Christmas Day. Rachel and one of my nieces wanted some kind of shoes called Uggs and an easy-bake oven, and they named some more things. Their list was pretty long. I couldn't really catch all my three-year-old niece was saying, she has her own language. My nephew wanted a remote-control car, video games and some type of water gun. I did enjoy talking to them and listening to the cheer in their voices.*

*My mother was cooking chitterling, collard greens, baked chicken, sweet potato pie. She cooked a lot. She loves to cook.*

*I found out on Christmas Day that the kids didn't get all the things they were expecting but they got some things they were enjoying. I could hardly get them on the phone to wish them happy Christmas. As you can imagine that was certainly the highlight of my Christmas. So in a nutshell that was my Christmas. I didn't do much.*

*It was nice of Martin to fill in for the village Santa after he got sick! I thought it was very parently/motherly that Martin's mother showed up to get her photo taken with her son Santa! It's obvious she was proud of him. I imagine he got a lot of joy out of being carted through the village and seeing all the smiles on the little faces. It put a smile on my face thinking of Martin dressed as Santa yelling: 'Yo ho ho!'*

*I'm doing fine. I got your letters, two of them to be exact, one from 21 and one from 29 December. With the holidays they were late, at least the one from 21. I still enjoyed them both, as the time it took them to get here doesn't really matter, the effect of them worked just the same. Made me feel very thought of and cared about, appreciated.*

*You're more than welcome for the cards I sent to you all for Xmas. And the thought of them being placed atop of the piano. I found it funny what you said about the piano getting crowded after getting the card and photo from Eoin and Róisín – and my card tottering at the edge of the piano about to fall off!*

Dear Ray, Here is an e-mail I got from a friend, Benny, who spends Christmas working in a homeless shelter in LA. He doesn't like Christmas in Ireland: too commercial, he says. We worked together in the Simon Community years ago, he used to be a plain-clothes policeman, didn't like it and left. He claimed once – with a laugh – that his gun was so heavy that he used lean over to one side when he was walking! Belmullet, which he mentions, is a place very near where Shell want to build the gas refinery in County Mayo. Lots of Irish people emigrated to England and the US right up to the '70s and after, and some of them became homeless. Anyway, here's what he said:

> 8.40 AM and it's still cold even though the sun has been up for an hour. This morning my job is to 'water the line'. It's a job I like. As I offer people, waiting for the kitchen to open, a cup of water, I have time to engage with whoever wants to. There are few takers before the rising sun begins to warm the day. One of the first is a young black woman. She is very obviously tired and says the water might help her to stay awake. I ask how she slept. She tells me it was cold in the car she slept in and that 'they stole my shoes'. Her feet are covered and I hadn't noticed that she is shoeless on the very cold pavement. Paul, who I know as a man who walks furiously back and forth, talks to himself. Fausti tells me that he eats and eats and when he can eat no more vomits so that he can continue eating. George, a quiet man who keeps very much to himself, who I engaged with on Saturday, tells me 'Things change when it gets dark'. He begins talking about the rats, then says he won't even go there and continues to talk of what it's like to try and stay cool when the police hassle him or when the dealers hussle. He knows how important it is for him to keep clear of the pipe and the bottle. 'Irish' John from Belmullet, who hasn't been home since 1974, doesn't show up. We had arranged to meet so I could give him the newspaper I brought with me from Dublin last week. Anne had called me from the kitchen to introduce us, he still has the *cúpla focal*, the few words of Irish. He gave me the address of his wife in Dublin and his brothers in Mayo and said to tell them he is alive and well. The last two people to leave the garden, an oasis of peace and beauty in the squalor and jungle which is skid row, are Asian Ron and a quiet anxious black woman. Ron is not wearing the stuffed penguin he used to wear all the time last year. He asks whether they fed

me on the flight here, remembers his father working with horses in Idaho and looks off into the distance as he intones: 'That's good, that's really good' to my replies. The black woman had been standing by herself for the last hour near the gate accepting only a cup of water. I ask what she plans for the rest of the day. Nervously she quietly says that she will go to the Woman's Centre but she is unsure how to get there. Jessie explains directions and I realise she is new to the row and is scared.

Another day in the Hippy Kitchen. These days the lines are not so long, more like a thousand meals served than the two thousand at the end of the month when welfare cheques are spent. The guests are the broken, the mad, the bad, the maimed, the lost and the found.

Outside on Gladys Street the dealers do a brisk trade offering a hit of six minutes' escape for a few dollars while prostitutes do their business in portable toilets.

Here the gospel comes alive and paradoxically in the belly of the beast I find a way to celebrate the feast of Christ in a way which holds meaning for me. Here I learn how to love better. May the Word of Christ explode in our world and in our lives!

*Le Grá*, With Love, Benny in Los Angeles.

*Here's a piece that I wrote a while ago: Not only is Christmas Day a day for loving, gathering and sharing, to me this day is also the most memorable day of joyous moments in my life. I remember waking up in the wee hours of the night waiting for the clock to strike midnight, Christmas morning. Waiting anxiously and excitedly, what kind of gifts have we gotten. Memories of being outside riding our new bicycles with friends and other children who had also gotten new bicycles for Christmas. These are the kind of memories that come to mind when I think of Christmas.*

*Memories of going to the store with my family to pick out gifts for other family members and friends. Or meeting at an aunt's house to feast with relatives. Everyone brings their own special prepared dishes, my mom cooking for two days preparing her own dishes of food. All the children in the house playing, laughing and sharing their gifts, while the parents complain about how much they've spent on particular gifts.*

*I hold a lot of dear memories of Christmas and they play a huge part in my handling Christmas on death row away from my loved ones. Christmas isn't the same these days around this place. The whole environment is a lot of depressed inmates missing their families and regretting the destiny that fate has set for them. But through it all there is always something to smile for during these hard times. For me it's my memories. Knowing that my loved ones and the kids are being blessed with the same joyous memories. That helps me through a difficult situation like the one I'm in now.*

*To everyone who reads this letter – Merry Christmas and happy New Year! Remember to cherish every moment and joyous time of your life, because there's no telling when you'll need the past memories to get you through a difficult day or time in your life.*

* * *

*So you don't shine your head! I just saw it gleaming in the photo you sent and I figured I'll ask some guys here who are bald with their hair all shaved off. They tell me that they add Blue Magic Pressing Oil to make their heads shine more! And so you pretend to be angry and chase your grandson, Eoin, when he calls you 'Baldy'.*

*Catherine and Martin is expecting in June, that's great news. Tell them I said congratulations. I thought it was cute Róisín patting Catherine's stomach and wishing the baby a happy Christmas. Róisín certainly doesn't seem to be just five years old, she's bright and smart. So herself and Eoin are practising their German and talking at table about how the German for 'six' sounds like 'sex'. I could just see all of the adults' faces and everyone trying to think of something to divert the conversation. Their lil minds pick up everything, don't it?*

*My Mom will be down in February when she's gotten her car fixed and everyone has days off from work. I'm sure you all miss Liam just as he'll miss you all while he's working in London. And thanks for sharing your friend Benny's e-mail with me about his Christmas with homeless people in LA.*

*P.S. Would you tear the stamps off my letters and send them back to me. I put glue over them that I can wash off and then use the stamps again. Something I learned while here. Shhh!*

* * *

*I'm sitting here now with my thermal and sweats on inside the cell. It rained last night and there isn't any sun out. Basketball isn't as common in the winter time as it is in the summer. Not only do our hands be cold and that makes it hard to shoot the ball, but also a lot of guys that play basketball don't walk outside when it's cold. We usually let the weather dictate the games. When it's winter I do more weightlifting.*

*The hall-runner work is going okay but honestly I'm tired of it, I think I'm going to quit or take me a vacation for some months. It's nice to be out of my cell but it's gotten old now and I want to lay in some, you know? Now that the second round of incentive boxes have been passed out, I get sent to the microwaves more often than before.*

*It's hard for the prisoners at this time, being away from loved ones, listening to the holiday music played all over the radio, watching the people in shopping malls holiday shopping. Those things are strong reminders of your missing out on a special time of year, so yes prayers for prisoners as well as for loved ones are needed. Loved ones suffer just as much as prisoners. Thanks for explaining what holly is, I'm not sure if I ever saw what one of them trees is.*

* * *

*Did I tell you the bad news? I had one of my appeals denied. The judge denied my petition, or rather granted the state's motion to dismiss it. So now I'll appeal the judge's ruling in another court and hope they do something. My lawyers tell me the way the judge went about it was wrong, he didn't deny the petition based on law. He basically said he was doing it in order not to second-guess the judge that presided over my case. This process is one that I truly hate, it's so frustrating to think about, it isn't one I'd wish upon my worst enemy. It's even more frustrating when you know there's good, relevant grounds that'll get me off of death row and the courts won't even pay attention to them. You have to endure these types of situations and try to remain positive but how is one to do that with the stakes so high? This judge has simply denied my petition, didn't read why I should get relief on my issues, and how or why we say justice wasn't served. Just because he wants to be honorable toward the presiding judge who held my trial. That's not right, it's just not right, and basically one has to just hope for more reason the next time round, you know?*

*I've went through my down stage of disappointment, I'm trying to stay positive. I've been listening to a lot of Damian Marley the last few days, he's Bob Marley's youngest son. There's a song called 'Road to Zion' that I love and 'Welcome to Jamrock'. If you can, listen to those two songs. . . .*

*I do agree with you, as a Christian one of the things that's certain is that God/Jesus does love us all the time, even more when we're weak and down and that love from the Almighty is certainly one to hold on to all the time.*

*I hope I get a chance to see my family this upcoming month, I honestly don't know if I will or not, I must not get my hopes up. My sisters have to find sitters for their children, which has proven to be difficult to do in the past. They used to come down with them but the prison made some rule changes that don't allow nieces and nephews to visit, so that's made it even more difficult. Rachel is fine, I haven't talked to her since the last time I told you. But I got a letter from my mother and she told me she's fine. I've been trying to get her mother to send some updated pictures but that's easier said than done.*

*I can understand the report you saw about the US soldiers on the plane in Shannon sitting there without much to say. I would imagine their heads were filled with thoughts of where they're about to go and what they were leaving behind and the danger they'll be faced with. That's a lot to bear.*

My apologies for the delay in writing . . . we got a new computer which just flies along but I had to wait a week until Tomás had the time to set it all up – that was much too complicated a job for me! You can even listen to the radio on it while you are typing.

We have been thinking about you a lot and hoping you are OK and able to cope with the court decision. I'm sure your strength will help you. You have shown yourself to be so positive and hopeful since I got to know you. Don't be thinking about writing, we will be delighted to get your letter whenever you feel able to write one.

We are all well here – I did some more painting in Clare and was exhausted after it – I'm not the man I used to be! Catherine and Martin were very pleased with my work! Martin is away for work all this week so we are going down tomorrow until Friday just to keep Catherine company. The area is so remote that she is a little nervous at night and Woody is no use at all as a watchdog. We will enjoy the few days, no painting this time, and the weather is improving.

The enclosed photo of Róisín is at the old computer. I said to her that she wasn't allowed sit on that chair because that chair was for the boss and I was the boss. She said she was the boss but that I could be a helper. Big deal! I went off and came back again but she still wouldn't change her mind. I went downstairs and after a while she came down and said: 'I'll tell you what, Daideo. You can be a helper because helpers get three breaks every day and I'll be the boss and you know the boss doesn't get any break at all!' You'd wonder where they learn all this wisdom!

On Saturday we went to a little family gathering for the fortieth wedding anniversary of Bríd's sister and her husband. It was very pleasant and I was the only one not taking an alcoholic drink. One time I would drink more than all of them put together (well, not quite!) and I didn't miss it at all. On 28 March Bríd and myself will be forty years married. We will have just a gathering of our own 'children' and maybe a party later because Bríd's brother, in whose house Saturday's party was held, has been diagnosed with prostate cancer so we will wait to see how that goes. Right now he is at the specialist to see what they will do. You can get radiation treatment or surgery to remove the prostate altogether. It is a difficult decision, I think. I have a feeling it is a little serious but we are hoping for the best.

* * *

*How are you and my Irish family today over in Ireland? I hope this letter of mine finds you all doing fine. I got your letter the other day and it found me doing fine. I enjoyed it as always.*

*Yes, I've been taking a break from the hall-runner job, there's somebody else out working now. When it gets warmer around here, I'll get back out, right now I don't want to be out there, it's too chilly. And I get lazy when it's cold. So I'm on break. It's not so much being tired of being at everyone's beck and call, even though that did get to me at times! And it do get cold here, but it's the kind of coldness what would probably be warm for you folk.*

*Rachel is doing fine at school but she had under-average grades in two of her classes, Math and History/Social Studies. She said those two subjects were hard and I basically told her, it's only hard because she's not spending more time learning them, or better yet, studying to make those subjects easier.*

*Well, Fam, I'm going to end this now, until next time. . . . It truly is a nice and pleasant feeling when I think and know that I'm thought of by such good-hearted folk as you all.*

From my teaching days I think lots of children find Maths more difficult than other subjects. I used to find that lots of pupils understand it in class and can do the questions in class but it's different after class. They all know they must learn off and memorise things in, say, geography, and forget that they should do the same in maths – that is, memorise the method for doing each different type of question. You don't have to rediscover the method each time. Just memorise it!

I used tell the pupils to never be afraid to ask a question in class, never let something go if you don't understand it. Is Rachel in a good class for asking questions, would the others get on to her if she asked a question? If so, she could always say to the teacher after class: 'Would you go over that bit again tomorrow, Miss?' At least that's what I used tell them.

Some kids are very shy about asking questions and if they do ask questions they are doing the others a favour too – you may be sure that Rachel isn't the only one having problems and lots of them would like questions to be asked that might clear up their maths problems. Maths will always be a little hard, perhaps, but that's part of the challenge. Is her maths teacher approachable, is it easy to ask her questions?

I think you are very right, Ray, when you say that study will make things easier. And I remember reading somewhere that educational psychologists (whatever they are!!) claim that study generates interest: if you study something you are almost bound to become interested in it.

History and Social Studies should be interesting and relevant for a black girl or is it given from a white person's point of view? If she got interested in that she might become a politician and leader?

Always feel free, Ray, to let your feelings rip with us when you are thinking about the legal system. We try to imagine your frustration and anger but we can't really know what it is like for you. In our life now it is only small things frustrate me – trying to change a wheel on the car, banging my toe off something, not being able to keep up with Cathal, politicians I think are cruel or just stupid and so on. But when something small happens I always say: 'Now multiply that by a million and that's how Ray must feel.' I always do that so that I can understand even a little of your pain. I always think that you are strong, Ray. Somebody on death row who is so positive and understanding as you – that is the most amazing thing of all.

*I don't watch much TV anymore. The MP3 is working perfect, I listen to music and the radio all day and night. If I do have the TV on I have the sound on mute and my loudspeakers on my ear. And the radio has a sleep timer and I set it to go off, 'auto shut-off', at 180 minutes and I listen until I fall asleep. Music is a safe haven when things isn't going right for me. Thanks again for this wonderful radio. The way you feel about your new computer is how I feel about my new 'car'. That's what we call radios here. Cars!*

*Thanks for sending the copy of the article from the* Irish Times *about that well-known death-penalty lawyer. Her firm tries to get a fair deal for those on death row. Her name is always on my appeal under my lawyer's name. She actually said while over in Ireland that she'd gotten some requests for penfriends and she'll post my name on to one of them to write me. Yes, I did tell you that newspaper clippings isn't allowed, it's good you were able to copy the article from the newspaper's internet site into your letter.*

* * *

*I'm doing fine. I just wanted to drop you a few lines before I go to bed. I've been up all day, listening to the radio, chatting to the guys on the tier. I went outside this morning and shot some ball. I had a very good day, it seems like I scored with every ball I shot. I have days like that where I just can't miss! I tore the skin off my right hand today, I tried to slam-dunk the ball and did it too hard. I've done that before when I get too excited or try to look pretty doing it! I'll be fine, it's nothing but a little skin gone on a couple of my fingers.*

*In my last letter I forgot to mention that I did get the BBC news article concerning the US wrestling with the execution questions. It was a very inspiring article. I have been hearing more talk around about the death penalty in the last couple of years than I have since I've been here, and that's a good sign. And just like the victim's mother that was speaking in Maryland in the article, the victim's mother in my trial was opposed to me getting the death penalty. Thanks for sharing the article. I do hope the state of Maryland abolishes the death penalty, it'll certainly inspire other states.*

*Oh, I have a couple of books I would like to read, actually it's five or six of them but we can only get two novels a month. You can order them from Amazon.com. I'm going to list them from the first to the last: 1)* Master of the Game *by Sidney Sheldon. . . . Remember we can only get two books a month and they have to be paperback. I'm going to go to bed now, my eyes are getting heavy. Take care. Best wishes to you all.*

Perhaps the huge cost of capital punishment compared to incarceration costs may be the factor which will tip the US away from the death penalty.

An Urban Institute study in the state of Maryland has found that the death penalty has added at least $185 million in costs to the criminal-justice system. These costs are over and above the costs of cases where no death penalty is sought. What have Maryland's taxpayers gotten for their $185 million? 'A system that has clogged our courts, delays justice for victims' families, and risks execution of an innocent person,' said Jane M. Henderson, director of Maryland Citizens Against State Executions. 'That money could have put more police officers on the street, put more correctional officers in our prisons and provided badly needed support services for the families of murder victims.'

The vast majority of death-eligible cases in Maryland have ended with a sentence of life or life without parole, not a death sentence. The study found 106 cases in which the state sought a death sentence and failed, cases that cost an additional $71 million to achieve end results that could have been achieved without the huge expenditure of time and money that is required in capital cases. Maryland has had five executions and has spent enormous amounts of money on a punishment that is almost never used. Vicki Schieber, whose daughter was murdered in Philadelphia, said: 'Not only does our state drag victims' families through years of painful reversals, but it does so at a cost of millions of dollars, dollars that could be spent on providing meaningful help to families so they can really heal.'

According to Jane M. Henderson: 'It's time to repeal Maryland's death penalty and replace it with the swift and sure punishment of life without parole. Maryland's death penalty is just another failed government program that is sucking millions of dollars away from the things our citizens vitally need.' At the time of writing, there are five people on death row in Maryland.

# 10

## Hammering Away at My Sanity

A young Traveller called here a few days ago. He had been in jail for drink-driving but after four months he got out on bail. He showed me the bail form – one of the conditions was: 'You must do what your mother tells you'! He's over twenty!

There was a lot in the papers here about the tornadoes in the US. We never have that kind of weather here. I heard that a couple of weeks ago there was a light-ish fall of snow in Chicago, nothing at all compared to the heavy falls they are used to. All the same, that day Mayor Daley had 260 (!) snow ploughs out on the streets – over-the-top, you would think, until you remembered that there just happened to be local elections coming up a few days later!

Today is Good Friday morning, a very quiet day here, many shops closed. It's a nice spring day. We will be thinking of you over Easter and wishing you strength and more strength.

*Since the last time I wrote a couple of unfortunate things have happened. First, I found out that the front office made a mistake and turned my visitors around, did not let them see me, after driving all the way over here, taking off work and spending their $ on gas. Can you believe that? I certainly couldn't. I was sitting here with my visitation clothes on, waiting, worrying,* *concerned about what may've happened. And then while sitting here waiting to be called for the visit, while sweating the clock as the time seemed to be in fast forward, they came and told me to pack up, they were moving me to another cell!*

*I had an awful day. I called, and my people – mother, sisters and Rachel – were back at home around 3* PM. *They'd already been here and for some reason they thought I was on restriction, which means I can't get visits. I couldn't believe that. My first time seeing my family in so long and something like this happens. I can't believe this and you know how long this has been something I've looked forward to. It's almost as if it's not meant for me to get a visit, something is always coming up.*

*This was an awful mistake by the administration and they won't even try to correct it, not that they can, but you understand what I mean. Now when I'll get another visit, I don't even know. I'll keep you posted. I must move on, the thought of this upsets me.*

*As I was saying my cell has changed. They moved my cell because the guy who was in this cell got into it with some of the guys over here on this tier so they switched our cells. I must admit the process of dealing with what comes with this situation is getting old, and it's really wearing on me, but what can I do about it? This is what it's designed for, to hammer away at my sanity and make me feel worthless and give up hope. I refuse to let them win, I feel I've come too far to turn back now or to let them win, you feel me? Not in a million years would I have thought this is where I'd end up. I've been here on death row for eleven years, incarcerated for twelve, came to death row at the age of twenty years. And this is supposed to be living. It's not, not at all.*

*The advice you gave concerning Rachel and her Math and the things she could do was very insightful. I'll certainly pass that on to her. You're right, memorising the method of the problem is all that's needed to be done with Math. And I do think Rachel tends to sit in class and not share with the teacher when she don't understand. She's not shy about asking* me *questions and I doubt if she'll be shy around her peers. But then again that's usually the way, a child gets shy when they're embarrassed to ask a question. I'm not sure if her teacher is approachable, I do know that she don't like the class. You stated her taking History and Social Studies may point to her becoming a politician. Naw! I hope not! Now a leader – yes! I want that to be her mentality all the time.*

'I usually just lie on the bed on the bad days and watch the walls and count the bars. . . . This is what it's designed for, to hammer away at my sanity and make me feel worthless and give up hope.' On the bad days, and even on the good days, the death-row prisoner is fully aware that the death penalty is not only about the minutes during which the prisoner is brought from the death cell and killed; it is about the death penalty hanging over one's head every minute of the day and, if they can bear to think about it, the prisoner knows that the search for a humane way of executing people has little to do with them and a lot to do with making executions more palatable to those carrying out the killing, to the governments that wish to appear humane, and to the public in whose name the killing is done. One has to be strong amid the daily horrors of death row. Some people are not strong, far from it.

In May 1989, the UN Economic and Social Council adopted a resolution that recommended 'eliminating the death penalty for persons suffering from mental retardation or extremely limited mental competence.' In 1997, the UN Commission on Human Rights passed a resolution calling on states to consider abolishing the death penalty and urging those states that still retained the death penalty not to impose it on people with mental handicap.

After years of outcry from the international community, in 2002 the US Supreme Court (*Atkins* v. *Virginia*) finally ruled that executing persons with a mental handicap was unconstitutional. The ruling dealt with the case of Daryl Renard Atkins (21), who was sentenced to die in Virginia for the 1996 murder of Eric Nesbitt (21), a US airman. Testimony about Atkins' mental abilities differed widely. Defence witnesses told jurors that Atkins was 'mildly mentally retarded' and functioned at the level of a nine-to-twelve-year-old. A prosecution expert countered that Atkins suffered from an antisocial personality disorder and was of 'average intelligence, at least'.

The Court banned the execution of those with a mental handicap, citing a dramatic shift in how state law dealt with such offenders. At the time of the Supreme Court decision, eighteen states had already forbidden the execution of mentally handicapped persons.

Catholic Judge Scalia strongly dissented and claimed that mentally handicapped offenders did know the difference between right and wrong. Supreme Court judge John Paul Stevens said that the execution of severely mentally handicapped people had become truly unusual, and 'it is fair to say that a national consensus has developed against it.'

The ruling came too late for the forty people with mental handicap who have been executed since 1976 and for the many more people with borderline mental handicap who have been executed since then. Too late for Jerome Bowden (33), an African-American with the mind of an eight-year-old whose execution so disturbed the Georgia legislature – the state known as the 'buckle' of the 'death belt' for its readiness to kill – that it voted to make Georgia the first state to prohibit the execution of mentally handicapped persons. When people see and know what the death penalty is like, then they reject it.

In line with international law, the execution of the insane – someone who does not understand the reason for, or the reality of, his or her punishment – violates the US Constitution (*Ford* v. *Wainwright*, 1986). However, constitutional protection for those with other forms of mental illness are minimal, and numerous prisoners have been executed despite suffering from serious mental illness.

James Colburn (43) had a long history of paranoid schizophrenia when he was arrested for murder. During his 1995 trial, Colburn received injections of an anti-psychotic drug that can have a powerful sedative effect. This heavy sedation posed the question as to whether he was competent to stand trial. There is the added risk that a blank or sedated expression on the face of the defendant may lead jurors to the opinion that the accused is without feeling. James Blake Colburn was executed in March 2003.

Amnesty International documents the case of Scott Panetti (49), who was sentenced to death in Texas in 1995 for killing his parents-in-law in 1992. He has a long history of hospitalisation for his mental illness, including schizophrenia, which caused him visual and auditory hallucinations. During his trial, Panetti – who acted as his own lawyer dressed as a cowboy – said that demons had been laughing at him as he left the scene of the crime. One of the doctors who was at the trial said: 'Scott was completely unaware of the effect of his words and actions. Members of the jury had hostile stares and looked at Scott in disbelief while he rambled on and made no sense.' Scott Panetti's lawyers won a major victory in the US Supreme Court in 2007 which allowed his lawyers to return to federal district court to demonstrate the severity of his mental illness and for the court to determine whether a man who killed two people understands why he received the death penalty. In June 2007, the US Supreme Court blocked the state of Texas from executing Scott Panetti, saying that he was improperly denied the chance to prove he was mentally unfit for execution.

However, a number of further court hearings were held, and on 26 March 2008 Federal Judge Sam Sparks found Scott Panetti competent to be executed, concluding that 'Panetti was mentally ill when he committed his crime and continues to be mentally ill today. However, he has both a factual and rational understanding of his crime, his impending death, and the causal retributive connection between the two. Therefore, if any mentally ill person is competent to be executed for his crimes, this record establishes it is Scott Panetti.'

After his original trial, two jurors stated that Panetti probably would not have received the death penalty had the case been handled differently. A further two jurors stated that if Panetti had been represented by an attorney, he would not have received the death penalty. One of them said that the jurors had voted for death out of their fear of his irrational behaviour at the trial. The atmosphere within the court was heightened by the presence of Texas Rangers on either side of Panetti, who followed him wherever he moved within the courtroom. The increased security may have had a negative impact on the jury.

A number of states have used drugs to bring prisoners back to 'sanity' in order to execute them. For example, in 2004, Panetti suffered from severe paranoid schizophrenia and was rational only when he was on medication. It was during an episode of 'drug-induced sanity' that the state scheduled his execution.

On 25 January 2005, Troy Kunkle (38) was executed in Texas although he suffered from schizophrenia and had to be brought back to 'sanity' by means of drugs. It was then legal to execute him.

The *Dallas Morning News* and *News 8 Austin* reported that the state of Texas, which comes first in terms of death-row executions and ranked forty-eighth out of fifty US states in 2005 in terms of the amount of money spent per capita in the treatment of the mentally ill, including funds for mental-health services in prisons, spends an average of $2.3 million to try a death-penalty case. In 2005, the per capita mental-health expenditure in Texas was $36.47. Only Ark ansas and New Mexico spent less, at $35.60 and $24.23 respectively.

I was so sad to get your letter about the cancelled visit. I hid it away so that nobody would see it and I've only just taken it down again to re-read. Bríd will read it later. I can't even begin to imagine how upsetting it must have been for you and also for your family. We had been so happy to get your lovely Easter card a few days before that and then to get your letter . . . but I am very glad that you told us what had happened. They say it's better not to keep things bottled up. . . . It's the kind of thing you'd read about in newspaper articles about prisons and then to have it happen to somebody we know so well . . . .

In your card you said about your life: 'It's not the best of lives but it's not totally the worst.' Your courage in saying those words left Bríd and myself more or less speechless and I think near to tears. You say in your letter 'I must move on' and I know you will. But it is very hard to have these kind of things happen to a good person who is trying so hard.

* * *

*I'm doing fairly well. I got into trouble the other week and I gotta go to jail, segregation for sixty days. Me and one of the guards got into a little tussle while they were in the process of shaking my cell down, searching it for contraband. They didn't find anything illegal but they was disrespecting my cell and I pretty much got offended and started arguing with the guard and I got heated. Long story short, I got into trouble and got wrote up. I got disciplinary action in other words. And that consists of not being able to play basketball. I must walk in a cage by myself, it's called the single-walk cage. Basically I'm not allowed to do things as the others anymore. I shower alone and walk alone. I can't catch the store or canteen for sixty days nor can I visit, which is one reason I wasn't tolerant with the guard. Anyway, I'll have to go to solitary soon this week or maybe next week, hopefully this week so I can get this from over my head. I don't like the fact that I have to share this type of news with you all but you would rather me be real, opposed to fake, I know already, and have done from day one.*

*I did get the novels you sent me, I'll take them with me. I'm not going to start reading them now. I'll spend some extra time listening to my music and watching TV, due to my going to be without my 'car' and TV for sixty days. I'll be okay, it'll take some getting used to but I'm good at adjusting. By the way I will be able to receive mail while I'm in the dog house.*

*I'll miss running up and down the basketball court. I miss it already to be honest, I haven't shot ball in four days. That was one of my pastimes, something that kept my brain tame. I'll miss it but on the same page I'll appreciate it more once I've regained freedom again. I'll try to write more poetry over there, I usually do when I have a lot of time like that. It'll work out so don't you all worry. I'll be fine, promise. Now to get to your letter.*

*I'm sure you all did enjoy the visit from the kids. It sounds like Eoin is turning out to be a great athlete. Five goals in one soccer game, that's good. I don't know much about hurling but it certainly sounds like he does – scoring in an uncommon way from one goal line to the next. He should be proud of hisself. As we are of his talent.*

*So what color did you paint his room? Oh, you say Róisín's room is a lurid shade of pink, you called it dazzling. I bet she'll call it the same. Dazzling! I'm sure she didn't like the thought of you threatening to transform her room blue! That's my favorite color, blue, dark or light, also green, grey, brown. Is blue the color you painted Eoin's room?*

*I was pleased to hear that your friends from Afghanistan are getting along well. That is a stupid rule, asylum-seekers not being able to work. Are they trying to push them towards crime? Well, I guess I'll end this now and let you go. I've enjoyed spending this time with you. Be sure to let the rest of the family know that they are thought of and I'm sending all my wishes for their lives to be blessed. I'm fine, just a rough patch, but will overcome it.*

We were glad to get your letter but very saddened to hear about what lies ahead of you for sixty days. I won't comment in case I make things worse, if that's possible, for you but I'm sure you know what I think and feel. We will be thinking of you all the time and wishing you strength and courage and the knowledge that you are precious.

We were out to see Eoin and Róisín a couple of days ago. They are very interested in the 'F-word' which they know they can't say! I told them that the F-word 'fart' was OK – in my experience children always think that is a very funny word! It shows you how little news I have when I'm reduced to telling you stuff like that!

I have got the address of a priest in the US who has a priest friend who is a chaplain in your prison – so if you would like to meet him, I can write to him. Whatever you decide. If the priest is a guy who has cop-on and savvy, it could be a little help for you, maybe, to talk to somebody who is not really part of the system. It might be a small source of courage for you.

* * *

*I got your letter yesterday and it found me doing fine. I truly enjoyed it. The feeling I had when I was reading it was a wonderful inspiring feeling, one I cannot truly explain in words. But from the bottom of my heart I sincerely thank you for your support and concern, it really means a great deal to me.*

*I honestly didn't want to share that news about segregation with you all nor did I want to write to you while in that state of mind. But I must admit it feels great to have you to share with. Thanks. And when you tell me things like you will share my thoughts and aspirations with your children and close friends, that is the most inspiring feeling of all. It's empowering, burden lifting, actually it makes all this feel worth it. You feel me? Do you know there's many out there in the world that would find our relationship strange? Booker T. Washington said 'a common thing, formed in an uncommon way' . . . . How about I get to responding to this letter of yours!*

*I just finished watching the video* Smoking Aces, *it's a good video, a lot of violence, it was worth watching, probably not something you'll watch. Besides that one we have this movie I know you will like called* Freedom Writers. *It's supposed to be good, about some inner-city kids attending high school and getting involved with writing. It's a true story, took place in California. They also have the video I really want to see,* The Last King of Scotland – *have you any intention of watching it? If so, know that my favorite male actor, Forrest Whittaker, plays the king. These will probably be the last videos I'm able to see until after I get my lock-up time out of the way, or I hope so, because I'm ready to get this out of the way so I can get on with things. It's no fun being isolated more than I am already.*

*I would have no problem with speaking with the friend of your friend, the priest here in the prison. But honestly that's not needed. I did find it amazing how small the world is. Your priest friend has a priest friend that just so happens to work in this prison. Wow! Again you don't have to go out of your way to acquaint me with him. Thanks anyway.*

*By the way is it possible for you to get me copies of the enclosed photos. Since I'll be in lock-up, I won't to be able to get Mother Day cards, so I'm sending out photos to my mother, sisters, grandmother and the rest of my favorite mothers! Remember you can only send me six per envelope – the guidelines of the mail room – and they cannot arrive all at the same time, so the postmark date should be different on each envelope. That's one of their new rules – a stupid one, but it's how they do it.*

Catherine is keeping well but probably a little nervous as the time, early June, draws near, but she is in good health. Last weekend they had Martin's mother with them. She is ninety-one, fit and well able to take a drink – or two! They went for a drive: Martin stopped the car to let another car go by, but when he went to drive off again he found the front wheel was half in the ditch and the wheel couldn't get a grip in the muddy verge. Neither Martin's mother nor Catherine were suitable people to try to push the car, so they decided to wait for help from a passing car. They waited forty-five minutes before another car passed along that road (your type of road, Ray!) but then that person went off and got his tractor and pulled them out of the ditch in no time. And as Catherine said: 'We got to know another couple of people from the area.' She's a bit like you, looks on the positive side and moves on. Martin's mother took it all in her stride.

We will be looking forward to your letter, Ray. We will be looking forward to hearing all the news you want to tell us. And for what it's worth, we think of you often every day. I say to Bríd 'I wonder how Ray is' and she very often says 'I was just thinking the very same thing'. We send you all our best wishes. Be of good courage, dear friend.

*I'm now in lock-up. . . . So one of your asylum-seeker friends has had his nineteenth birthday, I didn't know he was that young. He's a lad, isn't he? I found it funny you said he and his cousin are capable of running the country.*

*One guy here is on hunger strike, he thinks the guards are putting poison in his food. He invites them into his cell to fight. They don't bother him because he's not all there in the head. There are also what they call 'safe cells' for those guys who attempt to take their own lives. Then there's the Med Unit. There are guys there from off death row who had strokes and can't take care of their selves and there's three inmates that live there and take care of them and three others that come when the other three isn't working. And the guys in the safe cells isn't on death row. They have either life without parole or hundreds of years, they're from population.*

*I can't do much because of being on restriction but I'm not deprived as I could be. Between you and me, meaning no need to repeat this when you respond to this letter, but I have some things I can get through friends so my not being able to catch the store isn't a huge deal. If I need anything I can borrow it until I get out. I can use the phone if I drop my 'horse', a bag tied to a string, downstairs to one of the inmate nurses. I have Michael's number on one of the nurse's list so in spite of my phone privileges being taken, I can still get through, with their phones not being restricted. One learns to get by with outsmarting the system after so many years here. Oh yes, I'm being deprived but not to the point of suffering, so please don't worry about me here. Most of all I miss having the freedom to go play basketball. I can walk and get fresh air but it's in a cage by myself, while I'm on single walk. Hopefully, I'll be let off single walk when I get out of isolation over here. It's not mandatory that they let me off so I'll have to brown-nose or act as if they've accomplished their mission of breaking my spirits.*

*They don't like to see one not showing the wear and tear of the situation. I think when they see you're bigger and stronger than the situation you're in, it bothers them and they go out of their way to make life difficult, as if it's not already. I've really been faced with uphill battles my entire life and have had to conceal my true feelings or just be strong – if not for those I loved and who would be bothered to see me weak, then simply because if I showed weakness around the type of people I was raised around, they would take advantage of that and become empowered from my weakness. . . . I feel that's the way the warden and guards work, they push buttons and do things to steal one's joy, to demoralise. But I refuse to let them see me sweat and give them that pleasure. I'm accustomed to struggle. It's all I know, seriously.*

*You shared good news with the news of the big international award to Willie Corduff, the guy who was put in jail for ninety-three days for objecting to Shell's plans in Mayo. All the news you share is good to hear, whether it's about the grandkids or whatever. I'm going to end this letter now. It's shower time in about thirty minutes so I got to do my push-ups and my sit-ups. Say hi to the rest of the family.*

Don't seem to have much news. I spent a couple of days putting order on the garden, which is quite small, but it is taking this old man that bit longer every year! What is happening to you, Ray, seems very severe. Your description of solitary is what I imagined it to be but it seems much worse when somebody you know is involved. You must feel powerless. I think Gandhi used forgive people, and that puts the onus back on the transgressor – but that's not easily done. I was never in any kind of situation where I had to even think about these things. A prayer I sometimes say – much more in hope than in holiness, I can tell you! – is a prayer St Augustine wrote: 'Keep watch, dear Lord, with those who work, or watch or weep this day, and give your angels charge over those who sleep. Tend the sick, Lord Jesus, give rest to the weary, bless the dying, soothe the suffering, pity the afflicted, shield the joyous, and all for your love's sake. Amen.' I find that this prayer helps to take my mind off myself.

I think the prayers of somebody who is suffering like you would be very pleasing to God and also very powerful. They would – I am 110 percent sure – be much better than the prayers of people like me who have a comfortable life. They say – don't ask me who 'they' are! – that when people who are suffering as you are pray for others, it sometimes brings some ease and solace to the persons who are suffering. I think even at this distance I can hear you shouting 'rubbish' and other less polite words! I can't write down any of those words because I don't know them! I must ask Eoin! Yeah, I painted his room blue, three walls light blue and one wall a darker blue. How did you guess that?

I came across some hints for dealing with stress. Maybe they won't work in your extreme case but they might help a little – say 'rubbish' to them if you like! Breathing exercises – breathe deeply, breathe into cupped hands. Distract yourself – easier said than done. Delay – try to wait five minutes before you lose your temper. Write to somebody. Have a low-sugar snack. . . . These were from a book for addicts but I think the same hints apply to everybody really. Did I hear you saying rubbish – again?

The postcard I'm enclosing with this letter is of Glencree, about ten miles away in a quiet country area – I always go for the quiet places! The building was a British army barracks, then an orphanage for four hundred boys, then it fell into bad repair and was condemned. In the 1970s, when I was involved in the Simon Community, we brought a group of homeless people there on a holiday – I slept in the room marked X! We had a great time, bonfires, football, sing-songs, and you could see the people changing by the hour as they relaxed, but when the week ended there was nowhere for them to go but back to the night shelter and the streets. Nowadays it is a very peaceful centre for peace and reconciliation – all kinds of groups go there, including inner-city groups. We go there every so often. It is nice to sit in the sun there. It is the kind of place where I always think of you and I try to wish/send some of the peace of Glencree over to you.

* * *

*I know you're probably wondering why I was so eager to come to segregation and lock-up. Well, when you've been given seg. time and before you are actually brought to segregation, you automatically go to single-walk status, where all your freedom to mingle outside your cell with other inmates on the walk yard is taken from you. And your seg. time don't start until you're actually over in isolation. So I didn't want to be sitting doing dead time on the tier. I kinda expected to do some weeks of dead time, which I did.*

*Anyway I'm in lock-up, doing time. This time isn't all bad. Yes, bad because I don't have a TV or radio to occupy my time. I must find the positive in the situation. Things happen for a reason, and I personally feel like this is the perfect time for me to self-evaluate, and that's what I'll use this time for.*

*A friend has been trying to introduce me to another form of doing time besides the one I know. It's a more peaceful way of doing time, dealing with meditation. The name of the book he sent is* We're All Doing Time *by Bo Lozoff. I would like you to get it, if possible. The book deals with all kinds of inner-peace methods and gives answers to meaning-of-life questions. So far it's the most well-rounded book I've ever read. I would like to get your take on it, I think you'll like it. Tell me what you think of it.*

*Well, I'm usually reading or writing here if not working out. I try to do a hundred push-ups and a hundred sit-ups each day. Or sleeping. There's two other guys over here for different offences, one an assault and one for getting caught giving another guy 'special attention', if you know what I mean. This is prison. I'm over here for standing up for myself, but again this is prison.*

*There's been six or seven suicides since I been in this prison. About two years ago one dude cut his throat. Isn't that wild? Do you know I've never thought about killin' myself and I've experienced some pretty hard times and saw enough death and struggle to drive a man slap crazy.*

*I started reading* Master of the Game *yesterday. It's pretty good but I didn't expect nothing other than good from Sidney Sheldon. I'm 116 pages into this one, it's 488 pages.*

*Thanks for the postcard from the Glencree Reconciliation Centre. It looks very peaceful. I enjoyed the thought of you thinking of me and sending the peace of Glencree over to me! I certainly need it all. I would like to be able some day to sit out in the sun there, just in honor of you. Maybe even speak at a gathering to an inner-city group and share my story and what brought my attention to Glencree. I have a dreamy imagination, don't I? Some day, Uncle, some day . . . .*

*I was glad to hear you are all well. Cathal in great form in spite of his fall and the bump and black eye. You know it's a common thing for us little boys to end up with black eyes and big bumps on our foreheads.*

*I'll end this now. I still have an entire page of your letter to finish but I'm wore out. It's 3.15AM, the breakfast trays will be around in a little while, I'm looking forward to it, I'm hungry. I've been writing for hours, are you tired of reading? There's news that I nearly forgot to share. They have an execution scheduled for this week, the guy I don't know, but he has been here for over twenty years. Hopefully, he'll get a stay of execution.*

* * *

Liam was home from London for the weekend, he was in very good form and it was nice to have him here again. Of course, when he saw your letter he had to read it. I think he is interested because he is so near you in age. Anyway, he says: 'Ray certainly knows his own mind and isn't going to accept your opinion just because you say so.' That was one of the best things I heard about you! I think it shows you are an unbroken man of good spirit and may you always remain that way.

Your description of your situation seems so realistic and your determination to deal with it is truly inspiring and a good lesson to all of us out in the world. When I mention to people – not many, just good friends – that I am writing to you, I am never sure what their real reaction is. I think they believe it is a good thing to do but they are still unsure. . . . Our friendship is one of the good things in my life. Any time I ever reached out towards somebody less fortunate than me it always brought me great blessings. . . . I saw in the paper the other day that New Jersey may abolish the death penalty.

We were down with Catherine and Martin for a couple of days. We cleared away some undergrowth. You know the way the cuckoo has become so rare – in Ireland, anyway – that people love to hear him when he arrives every summer. We were delighted to hear him near the house but then for two days he 'cuckoo-ed' non-stop all day long. We sure had enough of him after two days!

They got a dry-stone wall built around part of the garden – it's a traditional type of wall where no cement is used. Different areas in the country have different styles. They had lots of big stones from an old shed which they knocked down because it had an asbestos roof which was toxic. They met a man who gave courses in how to build dry-stone walls – he had six people who wanted to do the course so he said he would do it in their garden and use their stones as long as they provided tea and sandwiches for the people doing the course. . . . So they have a lovely dry-stone wall for nothing, and Martin, who did the course also, now knows enough to put the wall around other parts of the garden. But Ray, if you saw how rough the ground is around the house you would fear for the baby – I think he or she will have lots of bumps!

*I can love what God can love. I don't love everything I do. But I love myself as I am because God loves me that way. I know I need to change and I want to change. In fact, I believe God is changing me daily. But in the meantime I will not reject what God accepts. I will accept myself as I am right now, knowing that I will not always remain this way. That's my main focus. Keeping this mentality isn't easy over all the years I've spent in prison. Trapped. As you stated, I'm an unbroken man of good spirit. I loved that, it really made me smile. It's always nice to know you're appreciated and admired, feel me?*

*They had a killing here and there's more scheduled for the coming months. They're throwing caution to the winds, it seems. I'm ready to go, get away from here. All the guys that got dates have been here over twenty years, the newer guys won't get that kind of time anymore. I'm really between the old system and the new system, the time frame is more uncertain depending upon the issues in one's appeal.*

*Wow! Six hundred cell phones found in Mountjoy and three flat-screen TVs. It surely sounds like a mount of joy and certainly the guards were turning a blind eye. That's very different from here. It's a rare thing to locate a cell phone here – that means segregation, jail time while in jail, like I'm doing!*

# 11

# CELEBRATIONS AND CONTEMPLATIONS

*I had a fairly good birthday, nothing to complain about, so that's something. And I got a lovely letter and card from you all, along with lots of others, some even from people I don't know, nor do they know me, but just did it. I was really feeling like the birthday boy around mail call. It is very moving to know there are people out there who don't wish me any harm and want the best for me. I like getting the cards from all over the world, wishing me a happy birthday. It's not a common thing that a person of my status is embraced and supported. If there was more that embraced such people as myself, it will make a lot of difference. I think a lot of people forget that we all have a story and we all have travelled the road of life. I was thinking about that the other day, everybody have a story to tell.*

*I was pleased to hear not only that Bríd enjoyed my Mother's Day card but also that it was displayed for all to see. Unfortunately I can't accept the compliment for the drawing. I didn't draw it, I bought it from another inmate who drew it. The new guy in the next cell to me, I will pass the compliments on to their rightful owner. I'm glad she wasn't expecting the card, it made the moment sweeter.*

*I just looked at my watch, it's after 6 AM. I'm going to go outside this morning so I need to get my hygiene in order. I'll get back to you. . . . It's now 9.30 AM. I stayed out a little under two hours, there's nothing to do besides walk around the cage and talk to the other single-walks. Anyway I'm about to get me a little sleep, I've been up since 9 PM yesterday and my battery is running low. . . . It's me again, 7.45 PM. I got me a nice sleep, which was intended to be a nap, but after I got up to eat lunch, tuna salad and French fries – forgive me, chips – I told the runner not to wake me up for dinner and I slept until mail call. I got a card from my hometown girl friend, she always sends me cards on holidays and on my birthday. I also got a new penfriend, a girl from South Africa. I've never written to anyone from Africa so that's going to be interesting. . . . Grace, a new Irish penfriend, in one of her first letters has taken me to the Trinity Ball, which truly sounds like an experience I'd like to have had. I've gotten a little too old to be partying like a rock star, I can feel it in my bones! Are you familiar with the Trinity Ball? And Powerscourt? And Johnny Fox's pub, the highest pub in Ireland? Another place that sounds like a place to visit!*

*Yes, they did go ahead with the execution and there's more scheduled. It appears they're trying to make room. There's been talk of there being other inmates that's been sentenced or going on trial on capital charges and there's not any cells here to put them in. There's talk that they're going to do away with solitary for need of the cells. I think that would be good, not that I plan to come back here anyway! But things happen, you know? Why do I think they're throwing caution to the winds? I think they fear the death penalty will not be around long.*

*Oh, I almost forgot to mention. Still haven't wrote poetry, I don't feel it. I tried to force it a couple of weeks ago and that didn't feel right to me. So still I'm just sitting on the dock of the bay! Ever heard that song?*

Your letters have been an eye-opener for me. The things you described – the guys near you in solitary, and your young days – are the kind of things I knew about in general, but it's much different when somebody you know is affected by them and tells you all about them. Many thanks for sharing from your very first letters your thoughts about your life – and while you might be angry about some things, you love your parents and there is no bitterness at all in you.

I'd say you're right when you say that your youth must have toughened you up in one way so that you would never think of suicide. In the time I've known you, the word suicide never once entered my head in connection with you. In Ireland, suicides run at over one a day – in one of the richest countries in the world – and very often people say of the dead person that he or she had no problems whatsoever. They must be unable to connect with other people, maybe, but your great gift, Ray, is being able to communicate so well with other people and to bring richness to their lives.

Both Francis and Catherine were at the Trinity Ball in their time – it's one of the big social student occasions where people strut their stuff. If you've got it, flaunt it. I get overcome with envy when I see the photos in the paper from the revels at the ball!

When he was at Trinity, Francis was cycling into town when part of his bike collapsed and he fell to the ground. He was very badly cut and scraped about his face – just two days before the Trinity Ball – but the girl he had asked to go with him, stood by him – why, I don't know, because he was bandaged and black and blue. Anyway, off with them to the ball. 'How did you get on?' we asked the next day. 'Great, I was talking to hundreds of people – I wouldn't have met them at all only they all came up to enquire about my health!'

Thanks again, Ray, for all your thoughts about your life. Regarding what you said about deep breathing and being conscious of your body and your breath, is breath the one thing all creatures have in common? I think how to perfect breathing so that you blot out all other things is learnt over a long time, and in a way it is the process rather than the product that is important. By the time you get this, you will be near the end of solitary. We will be thinking of you. When you get back, will the others have lots of news for you, gossip and so on?

* * *

*I'm doing fine. I have only seventeen more days before I am out of lock-up. I can't wait. I hope they allow me go back to the basketball court after I'm back in my cell. They don't really have to until they get ready, so I'm looking for some form of understanding from them. If not, it's still not the end of the world. Besides that, it's getting hot. It's annoying that you can't do nothing about hot weather. In winter at least you can put more clothes on or get under a blanket or even exercise to get warm. Summer without air-conditioning isn't my favorite season.*

*What you stated about my being able to communicate so well and how that brings good and richness to people's lives, I really felt good when I read that. You know I didn't do much talking in school. If I did, it was because I was either forced or was being clownish and annoying. How I was raised – having to comfort my sisters, having to deal with drug addicts on the streets, wheeling and dealing – knowing how to communicate was important. I was cut from tough cloth and I'm very proud to be a soul survivor, I can endure whatever. However, I'm only human, I will get fed up and stray, and when I do it's a wonderful feeling to know you all are there to listen. As you said, my story is that of thousands, it's very common but rarely is given verbatim in high definition, feel me? I've come to grips with a thought of when I write to you, it's far more than just a letter, do that make sense?*

*Jim, who gave me the* We're All Doing Time *book, isn't what I would call a typical Quaker, but how would I know? He's the first Quaker I've befriended. Anyway, his passion lies in anti-violence work. I'd say he's one of those that want to make a change in the world, he's for prisoners' rights. You would find he does lots of things to make a difference, or to try to make a difference. I think you'll find him interesting. How's Catherine? I'm expecting good news from you soon. It'll be a girl, I'm guessing.*

Summer heat on death row and in the general prison population can cause very real problems for prisoners. Some claim that the very way the authorities deal with the issue is in itself cruel and unusual punishment, as we have seen in Chapter 8. In recent years, a prisoner wrote from one prison: 'It has been so hot, I can only lay on the floor. I have asthma and take medication but it's hard to get to the clinic to see a doctor. I know people who have diabetes, and John M. has lung problems. Man, it's so hot, I can't see straight. This place is insane. . . . I am currently housed in a maximum-security unit which sits out in the open, which means the entire unit gets baked by the sun all day. Temperatures go into the 100s (38 C) a lot of days and sometime they even reach 43 C, so you can just imagine how hot it gets inside. The only thing prisoners have to escape the brutal heat is a fan which we can buy from the canteen. Other than that, there is almost no ventilation. Even with a small fan it's hard to breathe because of the intense heat. Recently they came through our building and stripped the power from each cell, leaving us with no way to run our fans.'

The high temperatures posed a risk of heatstroke or heat exhaustion. 'They haven't acclimatised themselves to the heat after years on death row?' a prison spokesman asked. 'They are only now complaining about the heat?'

How do older people look at life, you ask. I think you can sift out some things and put them to one side and concentrate on what you think are the more important things. Lots of the problems that were there last century are here this century and will still be here in the next century. I don't mean to disregard them altogether but just wish/pray they all turn out OK for as many people as possible, and then for everyone to move ahead.

You said, Ray, that at times you feel more alive now than when you were outside. I wonder is that because you have had to concentrate and figure out what is important and what is not so important. Working on the important things, in the light of eternity, makes everybody feel alive, I think.

I waver about life after death: yes sometimes, no sometimes. When I say yes, it's often because of good people who have gone before me: my parents, homeless people, my cousin – a nun in the US who died from cancer and who rang me before she died to say that wherever she was going she would hold me in the palm of her hand; she was a very good person. But all that doesn't make it any easier to be good. That's always a bit of a struggle and it doesn't get much easier with old age! But I suppose it's one of the things that makes us human.

* * *

*Ten more days and I'm free!*

*Do you want to know something I found to be funny in your letter? It was a boy! The card I have says 'It's a girl'. I'm going to still send it, we're family, we can share laughs. It's a story behind a card now, along with the sentiment of the card. Isn't it something that the baby was born on the exact same date as his great-grandfather?*

*Mail is usually passed out any time between 5 and 7 PM. After mail call and I read it, I may lie down and just think about all I just read until I fall asleep. Most times I get up at 9 or 10 PM and start writing up to 4 AM, breakfast time. They start picking up mail after breakfast time. When I'm not too tired, I stay up until the guard comes around to make sure he gets my mail. While waiting, I brush my teeth, pray and read my Bible. Those last two I wish I did more of, but . . .*

*Yeah, when I get back to my cell, the other inmates will try to fill me in on different things, catch me up on TV shows, tell me about the news, sports, what's new on the radio, things like that. You haven't returned stamps in a while, this is my last one. Please send some off the letters. Did you know postage went up to 90 cent?*

* * *

*I'm sending you one of the pictures I took during my visit. My mother in the blue shirt, my baby sister in the black shirt, the middle baby sister in the pink shirt, and last but certainly not least, my heart, my baby, Rachel, in the white shirt. I enjoyed every second, minute, hour with them. My baby has gotten big, she said she enjoys my letters. 'Daddy, I love reading your letters and cards to me.' That was the proudest moment of the visit. I truly enjoyed myself yesterday. We bought lots of vending-machine food, sandwiches, hot wings, things like that, lots of sodas. Rachel was ecstatic throughout the entire visit, I loved every minute of it.*

*Yeah, a visit means I'm out of seg. I can tell you I've really been enjoying being out of solitary and back free. I'm still not off the single walk or able to shoot ball but it's cool, sooner or later I will. As long as I'm not in lock-up, able to get visits from my loved ones and use the phone, that's the most important of all. Solitary is quieter and you have less things to distract you but distractions are welcomed more times than not, just to keep one from focusing on the reality of the situation.*

Catherine and Martin were delighted to get your card. We had a good laugh but we think you made a good recovery! If you tried hard you could think the word 'girl' on the card was just a misprint, a slip of the pen! The baby – a boy, Séamus is a boy's name, remember! – is fine, he was a bit underweight but is up to normal weight this week.

I know what you mean about the actions of children like Eoin being genuine. Eoin is exceptionally good with Cathal. Glad your birthday was OK – where did all the people hear about you? On internet sites? What do authorities or your lawyers think of that? Does it annoy them? I hope my letters to you, Ray, don't annoy anybody.

* * *

*You answered my letter perfect. You stated that my question about whether there was life after death was too deep for you! Okay! 'Yeah right' is what we say when modesty is being detected!*

*Have I told you about William D., who was executed back around 2002? He dropped his appeals, he wanted to go sit next to God in heaven, he truly believed that that life would be better. He'd been on the row for twenty years or more. We used to talk a lot about life after death. (The lunch trays are here. . . . It's not worth it, I'll skip lunch!). Anyway, William D. tried to convince anyone who'd listen that life in heaven was better and you should want to find out sooner rather than later. When I first got here, he lived about two cells down from me so we did a lot of conversing. Two weeks before his scheduled execution, he promised he'd return and give me a sign, which was to flick my light off and on six times, meaning it's everything he expected and more, two flicks means it's nothing at all like what was expected. And it's been over four years, no word, no sign from him yet. Maybe it's not meant to be known [what heaven's like] while [we're] here upon this earth, and his flicking the switch would be like cheating, huh? Do you think I'm wacky in the head now?*

*I like the idea of life after death being a continuation of our development in this life. You like it because that means we won't be just flitting around on shiny wings.*

* * *

*I hope this letter of mine finds you all doing fine, taking care of y'all selves and enjoying life. As for myself, I'm doing fine, just taking it one day at a time, keeping my head above water. I'm sitting here waiting to go outside, they still haven't allowed me go outside with the group to play basketball but there's nothing I can do about it besides sit and wait until they feel I've done enough time on single walk.*

*Thanks for the book of poetry by Langston Hughes. I'd never read any of his poetry but I'd heard of him on many occasions. I've read quite a few that I thought were very good. Do you have a book or should I write out the ones I like? Since I'm not sure, I'll write out a couple of my favorites. I read these out loud to the guy next door on Monday when I got the book. The first one is called 'As Befits a Man':*

*I don't mind dying –*
*But I'd hate to die all alone!*
*I want a dozen pretty women*
*To holler, cry and moan.*

*I don't mind dying –*
*But I want my funeral to be fine;*
*A row of long tall mamas*
*Fainting, fanning and crying.*

*I want a fish-tail hearse*
*And sixteen fish-tail cars,*
*A big brass band*
*And a whole truck load of flowers.*

*When they let me down,*
*Down into the clay,*
*I want the women to holler:*
*Please don't take him away!*
*Ow – ooo – oo – o!*
*Don't take daddy away!*

*I liked the one about 'Me and the Mule' and I also liked 'Hope':*

*Sometimes when I'm lonely*
*Don't know why*
*Keep thinking I won't be lonely*
*By and by.*

*I read other poems that were very defining to the times of his writing them. I'll share some more as time goes by. Again, thanks for sending this book of poetry. It's walk time, I'll finish this later on. . . .*

*After I came in from walk time, I got me a wash in the sink, washed my clothes and got me a nap until dinner, which was just bad. Anyway, while on my way out to the cage, I saw the officer that lets us off single walk. I asked him when he's going to let me off, he said sometime this week. Hopefully he'll keep his word but that's not taking place a lot around here when it comes to certain guards staying true to their word.*

*Glad to hear Catherine is regaining her strength and the baby is gaining weight fast. All the rain you spoke of that has the grass greener, I wish we would get some over here in the States, that would be a relief. The Irish people are trying to get away on sunshine holidays. I wish I could pack some sunshine up in a box and send it to you all!*

Nothing but trivia in this letter, Ray. We got the kitchen painted. Noel the painter asked what colour we'd like and I said 'Morning Glory'. 'I think that's a drug,' he said. So we settled for Morning Glow, a nice warm kind of yellow.

Talking of more medical matters – maybe I told you already – tomorrow we are going to meet a priest friend who the doctors thought had cancer and they cut away most of his stomach to discover he hadn't cancer at all. When they asked to see the hospital files, they were told that the files had been 'misplaced'! He's only (!) my age but can eat very little and needs lots of rest. He is accepting it all very well. People have great strength – mentioning no names!

I went for a stroll around the city the other day and met a fellow who is living on the streets – he asked me for a cigarette. 'I suppose a fag would be out of the question,' he said hopefully. We had a good chat: it was his birthday, 14 July, Bastille Day, and he knew all about liberty, equality, fraternity – the motto of the French republic. You meet very interesting fellows on the streets. Bastille Day is also Eoin's birthday, he is nine this year, none of us can believe it. I'd say you feel the same about Rachel.

I was reading a book the other day and came across a word I had never ever seen before. Dwam! What does it mean, animal, mineral or vegetable??!! Looked it up in the dictionary and learned that to say, for example, 'the dwam ended' means that you came back to yourself out of a daydream or a semi-conscious state!

The people in Mayo are still struggling away but I think it is too vigorous for me any more. Shell will not stop, I fear. One of the protestors sent me a joke about the people who work for Shell. . . .

A man went into a pub and had a drink and then he shouted out: 'All Shell workers are scumbags!'

A man behind him shouted: 'Don't insult me!'

'Why? Are you a Shell worker?'

'No,' he said, 'I'm a scumbag!'

You can see I'm hard up for something to say when I have to resort to (unfair?) jokes like that! The spirit of the people is high in Mayo so maybe they will succeed yet. The Taoiseach (prime minister) said he is trying to find a solution. I really hope so.

* * *

*I got up this morning to go outside in the single-walk cage but fortunately they finally let me off single walk so I'll be going outside with the group. I'm looking forward to that, as you stated I'll strut my stuff, not sure for how long since it's been a while. I know my wind won't be that long but I'll do what I do…*

*Wow! I went outside and played five games, the first game wore me out but I kept playing despite looking like scrap, that's what we call those players that can't play and need to be sitting out or doing something else besides playing b-ball! I had an okay day considering it's been a while since I've played. I made a couple of shots each game, it'll take about a week to get back to satisfactory play. . . . I came back in, washed up after I stopped pouring sweat, which took about an hour to do! And I put my ball clothes in a bucket to steep and went to sleep!*

*I did get the second copy of the Langston Hughes book a few days after I got the first one. I thought the company made the mistake and sent two. It didn't occur to me that getting the second book was because of your shaky hand that pressed the computer key twice! I was going to send it back to you but since you have a copy yourself and would like me to give the second copy to somebody else, I will do that. I have a good friend, Joseph, that likes reading such poetry so I'll give the second copy to him. I'm glad you have the book yourself, I won't have to copy my favorites down when I want to share them. I was reading it the other day and came across some I liked a lot. 'Trumpet Player', 'Midnight Raffle' as well as 'Island'. And there's one on page twenty-eight, 'In Explanation of Our Times', that one is the best I've read yet, I loved the realness of that one. I would like to know some of your favorites. There's all kinds of poems in the book, sad/funny/serious/angry.*

*I've had a letter from Grace, my new penfriend in Ireland. She's maybe going to France to study. She's having boy trouble so I've been playing counsellor for the last couple of letters, which is not a problem for me. I like helping out in the ways I can. As you know my helping is limited in my situation.*

Talking of books, yesterday I ordered the book you recommended, *We're All Doing Time*, I think it sounds like a title made up by a person who never did time. And still talking about books, I've finished Sunny Jacobs' book, *Stolen Time*. She was on death row for years in Florida and then put into population, lots of the book is about that time. Her husband Jesse was executed for murders he never committed, the execution itself was so botched up that his head went on fire. She was released in 1993.

She had a lot of 'freedom' to work on her case and the prison seemed humane in many ways. I suppose a women's prison would be a bit softer than a men's prison? There seems to have been a fair few kind officers in her prison. Lots of things she said reminded me of things you said, for example, her comments on the food!

Sunny, who now lives in the west of Ireland, said something that I found very encouraging for me. She said: 'We in prison depend on those we have left outside for our very existence. Without their support and acknowledgement we cease to exist in the outside world. We fade before our very eyes – we feel life slipping away as the people drift further away from us. It's like being shipwrecked in a hostile land, the land of the lost. And half the time, the people who supply you with the vital elements of life and hope, get tired or too busy, or simply don't care anymore. So, like the old Eastern adage about the tree falling (does it make noise if no one hears it?), we cease to exist.' That may be depressing for you, Ray, but for me it was very encouraging and inspired me to cherish and nurture our friendship.

I had an article, in Irish, in a newspaper yesterday. 'Twas a light article. Here's a synopsis: I saw a Guard giving a coin to a street busker. A miracle, I said to myself. The Guard was a couple of yards ahead of me as we walked down the main street. I definitely heard the sound, a coin striking off another coin. Even though the summer hasn't been great, still you can see great unusual things between the showers! Then I described a few more things I saw around the town, including a visit to the hospital to see a Traveller woman with a very big family, husband gone, she's just been diagnosed with leukaemia. She told me that she doesn't say much when she prays – 'I haven't the words' – but she always has great hope in God. And then I finished the article this way – I was happy that day on my way back to the car. I had cause to be happy because just a few days previously my grandson was born on the very same date on which his great-grandfather was born in Cork 108 years ago. I wasn't thinking at all at all about where I was going and with that my shoe hit off the collecting box which the busker had on the ground. I heard the sound, a coin striking off another coin. Oh, no! No, don't say that was what happened with the Guard. I'd much prefer to believe that he actually gave money to the busker. I'm sure he did. Didn't you, Guard?

Another major bit of news is that Bríd got a mobile (cell) phone. She wouldn't come with me to the shop to buy it, she feigned a headache and stayed in bed: 'You buy it for me', and so on. The fellow in the shop wanted to know was she confident about using the phone, and when I said nothing, he said his mother used to be like that but now she sends him texts every fifteen minutes telling him what she is doing. He is thinking of stealing it from her and throwing it in the river! We'll see how it goes. And I got a new pair of shoes, speaking of which – how are the basketball shoes holding out? I could post this letter now but the computer printer is broken! Grrrr, $*£"^&*, Grrrrr.

Professor Victor Streib, of Elon University School of Law in North Carolina and Ohio Northern University's Pettit College of Law, found that women are significantly less likely than men to receive a death sentence, possibly because prosecutors seem less inclined to seek the death penalty against female offenders. Prosecutors may be more sympathetic to women and more willing to plea-bargain in the case of women. Streib noted that women are charged with roughly

10 to 12 percent of the murders in the US but get about 2 percent of the death sentences and less than 1 percent of the actual executions. He also noted that it is impossible to know why prosecutors decide to seek the death penalty in some cases but not others.

Streib's report noted that: 162 women have been sentenced to death since 1973; in 1984, Velma Barfield was the first woman to be executed since the reinstatement of the death penalty in 1976; of the 1,099 executions in the United States since the reinstatement of the death penalty, eleven were women; the last execution of a female offender was in Texas in 2005; of the fifty-one women on death row, twelve killed their husbands or boyfriends and eleven killed their children. Two killed both their husbands and their children.

Since 1976, three states have dominated the execution lists: Oklahoma, with 87 executions, Virginia, with 101, and Texas, way out in front with 411 executions, including, most recently, the killing by lethal injection of two foreign nationals in one week: José Ernesto Medellin (33), a Mexican, on 5 August 2008 and Heliberto Chi (29), a Honduran, on 7 August. The International Court of Justice (ICJ) had urged Texas not to execute the two men as they had not been informed of their right to consular help when arrested. Texas argued that its courts were not bound by the rulings of the ICJ.

Speaking on CNN in 2007, Craig Watkins, the newly elected district attorney of Dallas County and the first African-American DA in Texas, said that the authorities needed to slow down the execution rate. Asked about women on death row, he said that the real issue was the fact that 41 percent of the people on death row in Texas are African-American, even though African-Americans comprise a very small part of the state's population. 'That point of view may be a little different from what you're used to hearing from district attorneys in Texas,' Watkins said.

Kathleen A. O'Shea, a former nun who now runs a pastoral ministry to death-row prisoners, writes in an introduction to her book *Women and the Death Penalty in the United States, 1900–1998* that when she visited the first woman she met on death row in Oklahoma, 'I was appalled at the conditions and utter power of men over women in these situations. I was sick for days after that visit, literally throwing up and unable to get out of bed. It was not because I thought these women are innocent, although some of them are, but because I was suddenly struck that these women were being held and treated in a degrading and dehumanising way. I was struck that prison officials are allowed to do this and to keep this a big secret, so to speak, out of the public eye, because the number of women on death row are so few. I thought then, well, I can't go open all the prison doors and force them to act more humanely, so maybe I can write about these women, tell their stories and put them out there so that other people can see them.'

Most prisons where women are held on death row in the US are in very isolated areas of the state where access is extremely difficult. 'Within the prisons,' O'Shea wrote, 'death rows, as such, are apart from any contact with the general population. Many women's prisons do not have death rows per se and so the women are held in isolation in areas generally known as "the hole". Very few of these prisons have any women working in these areas. The men in charge of women on death row have total control over what goes on there. . . . Women on death row frequently lack even the basic necessities. . . . These women aren't asking to be free – they are asking to be recognised as humans. . . . One woman on death row told me that the hardest thing was convincing herself that she was less than human, as everyone was telling her. But she felt she had to because she knew she would be in prison the rest of her life and to be able to survive from day to day she could not let herself believe she deserved more. I say, isn't it enough that these women have to live with the thought that they will be executed at some point, do we have to kill them every day?'

In its annual report for 2007, Amnesty International said that in May of that year Vermont became the last US state to pass a law protecting women in the general prison population from sexual abuse by guards, by criminalising all sexual contact between inmates and staff. However, many women prisoners in the US remain at risk of abuse through policies that allow male staff to conduct 'pat-down' searches of women prisoners and observe women washing or dressing in their cells. Most US states allowed male guards unsupervised access to women's prisons, contrary to international standards. Twenty-three states, and the Federal Bureau of Prisons, allowed women prisoners to be shackled during labour, a practice Amnesty International considers to be inhuman and degrading as well as potentially dangerous for the health of the mother and her baby.

*I think you're right concerning all Quakers not having the same view as Jim concerning the death penalty. He told me some of his friends he's told about writing to me have given him that stare and the question 'Why?' I agree that the situation is too much for some people, regardless of their religious belief. They tend to think solely on the situation or sentence, they assume that if he or she is on death row, they're horrible people. . . . It's not the easiest choice to make or think about when you're thinking of letting a criminal in prison or a convicted killer on death row into your life. So I guess it's understandable from those aspects but that don't make it right. There's a lot of judgemental people in this world and most of them don't take the time to know the people they're judging or to look beyond the surface.*

*I'm glad you enjoyed your visit to your brother and sister in Cork. Congratulations on your twelve months of giving up drinking. I do remember the time you gave it up. I was very sorry to hear about your friend, Columbanus. I read the obituary you sent. His account of the landing on the Normandy beach was very vivid. Can you imagine being in a place where battleships are firing behind you, thinking they're going to hit you, seeing the shadows of the shell going over? I can imagine his being horrified by what took place. He even said all those years later, after he became a Franciscan monk, that he got flashbacks and smelt death like it was yesterday. It's evident that the landing changed his views on war. He was certainly a very good person and very compassionate for others whose life was not perfect. He certainly should've been proud of his life and the things he accomplished on this earth. I'm glad you explained what the letters 'OFM' after his name stand for. I'd never have guessed 'Order of Friars Minor' but you also gave 'Order of Fat Men'! I think I'll stick with the religious explanation!*

* * *

*Have you got the* We're All Doing Time *book? I'm looking forward to hearing your thoughts on that. The book by Sunny Jacobs,* Stolen Time, *did sound like a good read. The story of her time on death row, the execution of her husband and how she is living now in Conamara. I'd like to read that some day. You wrote that she said: 'Us prisoners depend on those we have left outside for our very existence.' That is a true statement. I like how she expressed the things you shared with me. Yeah, I too think that the guards in a women's prison are probably somewhat more compassionate and considerate. It's obvious from what you said that their food was bad like ours. It would be a pleasure one day to meet her and share our experiences. You know I often think about what might have happened if I was fortunate enough to have met people like yourself or Sunny when I was out in the world. No, it wasn't depressing for me to have to read the things you wrote after your time spent with her book. The thought of it encouraging and inspiring our friendship is nice. You say you have read back over my letters to you – tell me, from your opinion, would you say I've changed?*

*You asked about friends I mentioned in some of my letters. My best friend, who got off death row and is now carrying the sentence of life without parole, he's doing good, he's down there in population, studying. Yes, we do stay in contact. He's actually to get married. I got a letter from his lady asking me for my blessings and informing me of her intentions for my lil bro. Stephen, the friend I told you about from my teenage years, is a different story, I don't know where he is, we've not been in contact for years. The last I heard from him he wasn't in jail. We were never in constant contact, actually before I left the free world we weren't that close, he was one of those friends that grows apart.*

*You asked about the hall runner's job and will I get it back. I doubt if that will be anytime soon. Solitary rules me out until they regain their trust in me. It's good to hear that Catherine and Martin and baby are doing well. I thought the advice you gave Martin funny. 'When a baby smiles, it's either fear or gas.' I'd never heard that before.*

Sunny Jacobs was wrongly convicted in 1976 of killing two police officers in Florida and sentenced to be the first woman to die in the electric chair under the newly reinstated capital punishment law. She spent five years in isolation on Florida's death row (at which point her sentence was commuted) and a total of nearly seventeen years in a maximum-security prison before being exonerated. Her children were taken from her, and her husband, Jesse Tafero, convicted of the same murders, was put to death in 1990 in an electrocution so grizzly that his head caught fire.

Sunny had been present at the crime, covering her children with her body in order to protect them. The person guilty of the murders was William Rhodes, who plea-bargained with the prosecutor. In exchange for a lesser charge, he implicated Sunny and Jesse in the killings. Though Rhodes failed a lie-detector test (and was the only one of the three who tested positive for firing a gun), the authorities stuck to the story he told them. They also kept the result of Rhodes's polygraph test from the defence – results that would have cleared Jesse and Sunny.

Sunny's book, *Stolen Time*, tells of happier days in the general prison population, where she 'revelled in the unimaginable freedom of eating in the company of other prisoners, teaching yoga and forging new relationships'. For Sunny, there was no comparison between life on death row and her new, more humane life in the general population.

What makes women easy targets for the prosecutor is often their unconventionality. It is claimed that juries will be less sympathetic to a woman who has lived an untraditional lifestyle or committed a crime thought to be unwomanly. Women, regardless of race, are often punished for being rebellious, sexual or violent, or for otherwise breaking the expectations of gender. 'If there is a common thread that ties the women on death row together, it is the fact that they have not lived up to some societal norm,' suggests Kathleen O'Shea.

Almost twenty years after her trial, Sunny Jacobs met a man who had sat on the jury that tried her case. 'He said that one reason they wanted the death penalty was that they wanted to make an example of a woman, and that would send a clear message to those criminals out there.' The jury eventually recommended a life sentence but Judge Daniel Futch overruled the jury – at that time, judges in Florida had the power to overrule jury verdicts – and handed down a death sentence. Judge Futch always kept a model of an electric chair on his desk!

In 1991, there were thirty-six women on death row in the US. In 2005, there were forty-eight, and at the end of December 2007, fifty-one – or 1.5 percent of the total death-row population.

# 12

## High-tech Crucifix

*They did have an execution here a couple of days ago. Matthew was a good guy, very funny. I'd had a number of conversations with him, we played dominoes together. Anyway, this execution was one like when I first got here . . . the day of the execution we, the inmates, used to kick the cell doors or shake the bars and scream, holler, just make moves. We've not done that for some years but we did it for lil Matthew. I liked that, he was a good dude, I know he would have done it for me, so I was one of the main encouragers, or rather I tried to be the loudest one. . . . They have more executions scheduled. I hope this pace slows down so much that it stops. A lot of the older guys' time is running out, some are twenty years or more on death row.*

* * *

*Sorry to hear your asylum-seeker friends had their case turned down. I do know how that feels more than I would like to. I agree with conditions the way they are in Afghanistan, they will not send them back. But one can never be sure with governments and their tactics.*

*How's Cathal getting on? That was funny about his father trying to teach him the word* fliuch, *the Irish word for 'wet', but Cathal finds it hard to pronounce the letter 'l'! I can just imagine him trying to pronounce it. I'm sure his mother wasn't pleased with his trying to say the word if it sounded like a choice word!*

*I've still not gotten back to where I was before I went on single walk. I'm starting to get there though, another week or two I'll be more consistent. Thanks for the positive feelings and thoughts you send across the Atlantic, when there's an overwhelming amount of negativity in the air around here. . . .*

*No, you didn't tell me that your daughter-in-law's aunt, ninety years experienced, was getting married here in the US to a guy more experienced than her. That's kinda unusual but I guess the saying is true: 'Love makes people do unusual things'! I hope all goes well with them both. They have a nice story to tell.*

Dear Ray, I was very sorry to hear that they executed your friend, Matthew. It was a hard time for you and as you say, more to come, it is hard to believe. Are the authorities trying to make it all so routine, part of the day-to-day run of things? Only for the Iraq war, there might be much more focus and protests about the death penalty but I think that time of protest will come too as George W. and his pals become more and more discredited. If the coming months are hard on you with executions, don't worry about writing. I will know you are letting the sadness pass over you, lying low on a bad day and maintaining your spirits as best as you can. We will be thinking of you twice as often during those times and I will continue to write just to show you are not forgotten.

I had a letter from my cousin in the US who has a friend who is a chaplain in one of the prisons. This friend said that in the prison where he works the inmates dedicate most of the week of an execution to the inmate being killed. According to him the prisoners on death row start on Monday with a prayer service on the walk yard and they do that all week. During that time they stop all sports, dress in their pressed whites, shirt and pants like the inmate is being killed in and they also wear purple ribbons. That's their peaceful protest. I don't know what prison he was talking about. When we were in California we saw San Quentin prison. I was amazed how big it was, like a huge yellow monster. Maybe that was the prison he was talking about.

I bought a nice frame for the lovely photo you sent us of youself and Rachel. I suppose she is back at school now? Tell her 'good luck' from me.

The lethal injection can cause excruciating pain. Since the first execution via lethal injection, on 7 December 1982, more than 900 prisoners in the US have been executed n this way.

The prisoner is strapped to a gurney, or what some people call a 'high-tech crucifix'. Even at this stage, problems can arise when the technicians insert IV lines into the inmate's veins. They often have to make repeated attempts to find a vein. In one case, eleven attempts were made, lasting fifty minutes, and eventually it was necessary to make a 'cut down' on the vein to gain access. We recall the prayer of Karla Faye Tucker: 'Lord Jesus, help them find my vein.'

There are other potential problems in administering the lethal injections: the prisoner may resist and delay establishment of an intravenous line, the mixture or composition of drugs may be wrong, the direction of flow of the injection may be wrong, the chemicals may be directed into tissue rather than into a vein, and the prisoner may not react normally to the drugs.The technicians who perform lethal-injection executions must have the expertise to insert IV lines, mix and administer drugs, monitor the IV lines, monitor the prisoner's level of consciousness, and be able to react quickly to rectify at any stage in the process any error which might lead to a torturous execution.

Capital punishment is rejected on ethical and professional grounds by the American Medical Association, the American Nurses' Association, the American College of Physicians, the American

Public Health Association, the National Association of Emergency Medical Technicians, the American Society of Anaesthesiologists, and the Society of Correctional Physicians. Capital punishment in any form is not the practice of medicine. However, health professionals are required by law in many death-penalty states to assist executions.

In California in February 2006, two anaesthetists refused to monitor the administering of a barbiturate designed to render unconscious convicted killer Michael Morales (47) before he was to be killed with two other drugs. Two hours before the scheduled execution, the State of California announced that it could not comply with a lower federal judge's ruling that the execution must be carried out by a medical professional due to the type of drugs being used in the execution. As licensed physicians are ethically prohibited from participating in executions, California indefinitely suspended Morales's execution. Death-penalty opponents cheered; a moratorium on capital punishment is currently in place in California. The debate over the ethics of medical professionals' involvement in the officially sanctioned ending of human life got a little hotter.

On 30 June 2008, the California Commission on the Fair Administration of Justice (created by the California State Senate) released a report on the death penalty which revealed that California's death-penalty system is excessively costly and riddled with problems, which lead to wrongful convictions and a lack of fairness. At the same time in Tennessee, the Committee to Study the Administration of the Death Penalty (created by the Tennessee legislature in 2007) is also looking at many issues relating to the death penalty in Tennessee, including problems with accuracy, fairness, the way in which people with mental illness and mental retardation are treated by the system, and the services provided for both victims' families and families of those who are executed. It is reported that the committee has found that the Tennessee system features many flaws that are similar to those found by the California Commission.

The lethal injection consists of three drugs. The first of the drugs to be administered is sodium thiopental, a fast-acting anaesthetic that is intended to cause unconsciousness.

The second drug is pancuronium bromide, which causes paralysis of all muscles, including the diaphragm, which controls breathing. This drug is not a sedative and does not affect the ability to feel pain. If the inmate is still conscious when this second drug is administered, he will experience the physical and mental agony of suffocation, but if he is paralysed he will not be able to show that he is suffocating to death. The drug can hide evidence of consciousness.

The third drug is potassium chloride, which is intended to bring about death by stopping the heart. There is medical agreement that if the inmate is not unconscious, the intravenous injection of this drug causes excruciating pain, as if the person's veins have been set on fire.

The Berkeley Law Death Penalty Clinic says that lethal injection with the three-drug formula presents serious risks of causing severe pain for the person being executed: 'Its administration is a complicated procedure that requires placing the inmate in a deep anaesthetic state with the first drug to ensure that the inmate does not consciously experience paralysis and asphyxiation caused by the second drug or the excruciating pain of cardiac arrest caused by the third drug.'

Because of the potential for masking pain, the American Veterinary Medical Association has rejected the use of paralysing agents like pancuronium bromide in animal euthanasia. The AVMA guidelines dictate that the use of potassium chloride – that is, the third drug which is administered during lethal-injection executions – is unacceptable and 'absolutely condemned' unless the animal is in a surgical state of anaesthesia.

The Berkeley Law Death Penalty Clinic says that because of the use of pancuronium bromide and the failure of the authorities to collect relevant data, it is impossible to know how many lethal-injection executions have been inhumane.

* * *

*I've not really had the chance to sit down and talk with Joseph, my friend who I gave the poetry book to, but I have talked to him and he's pleased. Just like me, he'd heard of Langston Hughes but had never read any of his work. . . . I get to talk to him when I go outside and pass by their windows.*

*It's my old tier, so I'm usually hollering at some of them, and I ask Joseph which one he found that he likes.*

*I've found some others that I like. Every time I find a favorite, I find one I like more. 'Freedom Train', also 'Refugee in America', that's the realest I've ever read, it's beyond factual. Another one I like a lot is 'Life is Fine'. I found it funny what you said about hearing the black accent. You're right, you can hear the accent from the poems. Just like you, I would like to learn lots of the poems by heart but that's going to take a while, my memory isn't that good either. I've read some of the 'Madam to You' poetry, I found a lot of humor in those, like 'Madam and the Rent Man'. These are sassy, defiant, yet humorous. Like you, I think the book is as good as any thesis for giving an idea of what it's like to grow up as a black person.*

*I got some news for you. I now wear a bald head all over. It was getting too thin on top so I've decided to shave it all off, so now I'm skinned bald, I have a cue ball like you! As soon as I can, I'll take some pictures for you!*

*I got your letter the other day and it found me doing fine. I enjoyed it, as always. I'll pass on your repeat advice to Rachel about keeping her head down and to work hard and quietly and to ask questions if she doesn't understand. I will send her a letter this week with exactly your advice enclosed.*

*And you had another big family lunch! It would have been nice to be there and especially to meet your son, Liam, home from London for the weekend. I would like to get to know him, as he's about my age I think we'll have something in common, or I'd like to find out.* No Homo! *In here when we say things such as I said about another guy we say 'no homo' to let it be known there's no funny business going on. I wonder if you've gotten that* We're All Doing Time *yet and what do you think of it and so forth.*

In 1987, lawyers representing Georgia death-row inmate Warren McCleskey took the issue of racism and the death penalty to the US Supreme Court. McClesky's lawyers analysed Georgia's sentencing procedures. Their study examined more than two thousand murder cases. After accounting for variables such as the previous criminal record of the defendant, the study concluded that the odds of a death sentence in cases in which blacks killed whites were as much as eleven times higher than in the capital murder of a black victim by a white person.

The Supreme Court accepted the validity of most of the study's findings but ruled that 'apparent disparities in sentencing are an inevitable part of our criminal-justice system'. In a 5–4 opinion written by Justice Lewis Powell, the majority maintained that statistical proof of bias in the sentencing process as a whole was not grounds to reverse an individual sentence, nor did this statistical evidence invalidate the state's sentencing procedures. Therefore, the Court ruled, the evidence presented in the appeal had failed to demonstrate that McCleskey, a black man found guilty of the murder of a white police officer in 1978, was treated unjustly when he was condemned to death. To succeed, an accused must prove that racial prejudice animated his judge, his prosecutor or his jury. Short of an admission of racial bias by the prosecutor or jurors, this burden of proof is almost impossible to meet.

So Warren McCleskey's lawyers proceeded to prove something else, which was also alarming: Georgia prosecutors had obtained the most damaging evidence against him – his alleged admission that he was the triggerman – from a jailhouse informant who had been planted by Atlanta police, in violation of McCleskey's rights. The state hid the informant's status for a decade, stonewalling defence attempts to throw out or discredit his testimony. In April 1991, the Supreme Court ruled 6–3 that McCleskey's lawyers had waited too long to raise the informant's identity, even though they lacked the proof of identity – which the state was hiding – at the time when they were supposed to raise it. Then, just days before the scheduled execution, two former jurors told the Georgia Board of Pardons and Paroles that their votes to sentence Warren McCleskey to death would have been different had they known that the informant was a police plant, with an incentive to bargain for leniency in his own criminal case. Too late. The only other evidence that McCleskey had been the gunman came from an accomplice to the robbery. All four hold-up men were legally responsible for the killing, no matter who pulled the trigger, but McCleskey was the only one executed – on evidence that was illegally obtained, incomplete and questionable.

The McCleskey ruling and other Supreme Court rulings since then have, according to Sr Helen Prejean, so restricted appeals that death-row petitioners can be confronted with many technical barriers, such as no hearing for appeals that are lodged just one day late – this in a case of life or death.

Several years later, Justice Powell admitted that he hadn't fully understood the statistical evidence of prejudice in the McClesky case and wished that he had voted differently. He said: 'I have come to think that capital punishment should be abolished.' This change of heart came too late for McCleskey, who was executed in 1991.

In 1972, as we have seen, the US Supreme Court (*Furman* v. *Georgia*), in a 5–4 decision, struck down all death sentences because it found them to be inconsistent and profoundly unfair, with evidence of racial bias.

Four years later, the Court (*Gregg* v. *Georgia*) sanctioned new capital-punishment statutes that promised equal justice. The first execution after the 1976 reinstatement of the death penalty was that of Gary Gilmore. He waived all his appeals and died by firing squad in Utah on 17 January 1977. His last words were: 'Let's do it.' Since then, more than 5,000 people have been sentenced to death and over 1,100 executions have been carried out.

Despite the Court's assurances of equity and its promise of punishment determined with fairness and with special guidelines, bias – in particular racial bias – remains at the centre of the death-penalty system. US Supreme Court Justice Harry Blackmun, who had sided with the majority in Gregg, said: 'This twenty-year death-penalty experiment has failed.' Racism was central to Blackmun's determination: 'Even under the most sophisticated death-penalty statutes, race continues to play a major role in determining who shall live and who shall die.'

A 1990 US General Accounting Office report revealed 'a pattern of evidence indicating racial disparities in charging, sentencing and imposition of the death penalty'. In its 1997 call for a moratorium on executions, the American Bar Association concluded that 'racial discrimination remains in courts across the country'.

Amnesty, the American Civil Liberties Union (ACLU), the Death Penalty Information Center and researchers in the Universities of North Carolina and Iowa have published the results of their studies into racism in the operation of the death-penalty system in the US. They have found that people of colour comprise 43 percent of total executions since 1976, while comprising only around 25 percent of the population (ACLU, 2003). Since 1976, blacks and whites have been the victims of murders in almost equal numbers, yet 80 percent of the people executed in that period were convicted of murders involving white victims. While they made up 12 percent of the population (2003), African-Americans accounted for 43 percent of death-row inmates (Amnesty International).

The jurisdictions with the highest percentages of minorities on death row are: US Military (86 percent), Colorado (80 percent), Louisiana (72 percent) and Pennsylvania (70 percent). In North Carolina, the odds of receiving a death sentence rose by 3.5 times among those defendants whose victims were white, and the odds of receiving the death penalty in Philadelphia increased by 38 percent when the accused was black.

At trials during the 1980s, prosecutors in Georgia sought the death penalty for 70 percent of black defendants with white victims, but for only 15 percent of white defendants with black victims. Between 1983 and 1993, prosecutors in Philadelphia voted to remove 52 percent of potential black jurors while trying to remove only 23 percent of other potential jurors.

Race was also a decisive factor in juvenile death entences. Over 60 percent of persons sentenced to death for childhood offences since 1976 have been either African-American or Latino. Almost two-thirds of juvenile offenders on death row were persons of colour. Of twenty-one juvenile offenders executed in the US since 1976, 57 percent were either African-American or Latino. The only other countries that allowed the execution of juveniles were Iran, Nigeria, Pakistan, Saudi Arabia and Yemen. Bad company for the US? On 1 March 2005, the US Supreme Court ruled that the execution of juveniles was unconstitutional.

In 2003, Amnesty International said that since the US ratified the International Convention on the Elimination of All Forms of Racial Discrimination in 1994, the courts and legislatures in the US have failed to act decisively in the face of evidence that race has had an impact on capital sentencing. At the same time, Congress has gutted public funding of legal-aid services for death-row prisoners – which, for most, constitute their only legal representation.

* * *

I got a haircut too! But not an extreme one, just tight – it makes me look younger, Bríd says. I only look about seventy now! Did I tell you, Ray, that it was Bríd's turn last week to fall and hurt her ribs. It's true, I am not joking. I was out, I can't even go out now! She was reading the paper, sipping a cup of tea, all was right with the world. She went to get up and caught her legs in the legs of the chair – she thinks – and down with her! She eventually agreed to go to the doctor, who gave her tablets. Much improved now but still a little sore, nothing broken we think, but even if the ribs had been broken, they just say 'Let them heal themselves'. At least it made her go to the doctor, which she hasn't done for years. . . .

I nearly forgot – I have a story, I like to call it a 'novel', half-written, in Irish, about Travellers, but I can't concentrate on finishing it. So for three weeks I'm renting the house in Conamara we went to last May to see if I can finish it. I was going on my own but now I think Bríd has decided to come as well. I kind of have all the characters on the stage but for the life of me I don't know how I'm going to get them off, if you know what I mean! I won't have the computer and printer, so for a few weeks I'll only be able to send you postcards of lonely/remote/empty/dreary/deserted/rural/quiet/rustic/misty parts of Ireland – I hope you don't mind, Ray! It doesn't mean we'll be thinking of you any the less. I don't think I'll succeed in making a breakthrough on the 'book' but we'll see!

* * *

*I've had a rough week. My visit with Jim didn't go down because I didn't get the visitation list back in time so we put it off. That was something I didn't want to happen, I was really looking forward to the visit.*

*And then I've been very worried about Michael. I've been unable to get in touch with him and that's very unusual. The last time I talked to him, he wasn't in the best of spirits, he wasn't in the best of health either. Now I can't get in touch with him, I don't know what to think, I hope all is well with him. He's been a very loyal and dedicated friend to me over the years, one I've grown very dependent upon to be there, so I'm sure you can imagine this is stressing me out, and I don't know what to do to find out or get in touch with him or anybody that could give me any news concerning him.*

*I liked the postcards you sent and thanks for the letter. I thought the postcard of Glendalough was nice, the skyline of trees is beautiful. And I found it funny you said you saw the postcard of the farmer with the donkey carrying the milk to the creamery and you immediately thought of me! Yes, another postcard from you showing another empty road! If I didn't know any better, I'd think there was nothing in Ireland but empty roads. I didn't know Ireland was called the 'Land of Saints and Scholars'. I got a lot of history lessons taught in this letter of yours. . . . And then why the round towers were built. That was a very smart and well thought-out plan by the monks. I bet those Vikings was taken aback when they first realised they'd been outsmarted, huh?*

*I've come to the end of this letter. I'm going to close now and finish this in the morning. I'll get some sleep but before I do I must admit that spending this time writing to you helped me ease my mind and do something other than worry. Thanks. . . .*

*Good day! How are you? I'm doing very well! Guess what? I talked to Michael this morning, finally after two weeks, finally. He said he was in the hospital for those two weeks with some illness. I was so very glad to know he'd not passed away on me, as I was thinking. I could have jumped and done a backward flip right here in the cell! When I first heard his voice after accepting his call, he knew I'd been worrying. I told him from now on he needs to have someone contact me if something of this sort ever happens again. As you can imagine, I feel good right now.*

* * *

*Just got another letter from you. I found it funny what you said about Cathal with his shovel, saying he's a working man! Tell him to be patient, his time is coming, he'd better enjoy the pleasures of being taken care of while he can, huh?*

*Do you ever miss not working? Michael may have to retire soon, he's not well. I will have to find somebody dependable to forward to me the $ you send, Michael's having trouble getting out now. He's been a very reliable friend, loyal and wise, my very first penfriend. He's getting old, I remember he used to go get copies of pictures for me, books, radios, whatever, now he's barely getting around. Time changes things, don't it? He's a great friend, I'll be forever in debt to him, he's never let me down, never. You don't meet many friends like him.*

*I was pleased to hear that Bríd was doing fine and her ribs wasn't hurting. What's she doing over there, playing rugby or something of the sort? She just refused to heed my cries of 'Take Care', huh? I'm glad she's not seriously hurt and nothing was broken in the fall.*

*I enjoyed the snippets about George W. Bush from his new book. Of course, he should be crying and shedding tears when he's reading casualty reports from Iraq. I don't think his tears are true tears, he's just trying to clean up his image before he leaves office. He's never shown much concern about killing, why now? And his faith in God, well, let's not go there.*

*It's funny you spoke of seeing references to Langston Hughes since you got his book. I did too in an African-American magazine,* Ebony, *where he was referred to as the best black poet. He's well respected in our culture. They also mentioned George Jackson's* Blood in My Eye *and* The Soledad Brothers, *could you get those for me, please, if you can locate them. The Langston Hughes poem you sent me that isn't in the book, I liked that. I cut it off the page and glued it on the door of my tray trap:*

*Hold fast to dreams*
*For if dreams die*
*Life is a broken winged bird*
*That cannot fly.*

*Hold fast to dreams*
*For when dreams go*
*Life is a barren field*
*Frozen with snow.*

Back again in Dublin from my three weeks in Conamara, County Galway. Very remote, at night no artificial light at all, pitch black, which made the sky full of stars that seemed brighter than I had ever seen them. A lovely lake just fifty yards away, beautiful changing colours at this time of year. For the first time ever I cooked for myself and used the washing machine – no problem! I'm so proud of myself!

Bríd came over from Dublin for a few days in the middle, and Catherine and baby Séamus came for two nights. . . . That was a nice break from the cooking for me! The best thing for me was that in the solitude I got my story more or less finished. I could never have done that here in the city. I heard a writer – I was going to say 'another writer' – say that you can write an article at home but to write a book you must go away.

Rahim and Hamid, our Afghan asylum-seeker friends, were here the other day. They are well out of the horrible hostel they were staying in. A report came out during the week about centres here for asylum-seekers. It said that some of the centres are so damp that there are mushrooms growing in the corridors! They still have no news about whether they can stay in Ireland or not but in the meantime they say that people are being really nice to them.

Ray, I hope you don't mind me saying this but I am a bit uneasy about not sending money via Michael any more. I had an e-mail from him and he seems a bit down about getting old, even though he is five or six years younger than me, and I fear he may get worse if people imply in any way at all that he is getting too old. I think he needs a bit of a boost and I think one thing that we could do for him is to let him handle any money from me until he tells me to stop, even if it's only to make him feel useful and valuable. I think it would be a good deed you could do – that probably sounds pompous.

I was thinking too about what you said in your last letter. I know you will be careful but I think you should be very sensitive in this matter of him being able to pass $ from me on to you. It would be terrible to hurt him in any way. I think I would leave it largely up to himself. Say something like: 'Would you like to give up some or all of what you are doing for me? Is it getting too much for you?' and if he says it's OK, I think I would let it go on as now on the understanding that he will let you know if/when it gets too much for him. Remember too that doing things for you is probably also good for him – until it gets too physically demanding for him.

As I understand it, your phone calls to him are collect, which means he pays, I think? Are you sure this cost isn't too much for him? I think he is not that well off. Don't do anything rash. Michael is tried and tested and trusted. It could be very hard to get somebody else that would be as good. And above all else he is your friend. Before you decide to say anything, draw deep breaths, delay and wait another few days to see what you think then. Hope you don't mind me saying all this. I think it's better to say it.

* * *

*I'm fine. I've been doing the same old thing, playing ball and yes, I've regained my old form, I'm seriously hard to stop now, it takes two and sometimes three people to do that. And I have my wind back, I can run up and down the court all day now.*

*You sounded like you had a great adventure in County Galway while you were trying to finish your book. The Conamara night sky, the stars shining brighter than you've ever seen them, the lake, the trees changing in the fall weather. And you should be proud of yourself, cooking for yourself and able to use the washing machine! I'm impressed that you figured out the washing machine, since you have trouble ordering books with that shaky hand of yours. . . .*

*I started this letter Thursday but decided to wait until the weekend to finish it. I knew I was going on the visiting yards on Friday to meet Jim. He got to the prison safe, arrived 8* AM *and stayed until 1.30* PM. *He said he enjoyed himself, I certainly did. We ate and enjoyed some good laughs. My mother and sisters are coming towards the end of the month.*

*Michael isn't physically able to do the things he used do for me. When I explained about finding somebody else to do those things, he understood, it's really me looking out for his best interest. I certainly did not do anything rash and I know he is tried, tested and trusted. And no, I didn't mind at all you saying what you said about love being a two-way thing and that I should now show love for Michael, who has always shown me love, by continuing to let him pass the $ on to me and that would help his self-esteem. You have more than a right to say what you feel. I would always rather you do that.*

*What did you think of* We Are All Doing Time*? Bríd said she was enjoying it and that made me happy. I told Jim you all said you were going to enjoy the book.*

Many thanks for great letter received today. First of all, thanks for explaining about Michael and I hope you were not hurt by what I said in my last letter. I know you are his friend too. I sent

$ to him yesterday and I can send future $ to Jim and now and again to Michael so that he doesn't feel left out. That might be important in his present low state?

* * *

*I'm doing fine. This past weekend I attended a spiritual retreat given by a faith-based group, it took place for three days, members of that group go around to all the prisons. They are a Christian-based group of men who came to share about their lives from the low points to when it changed. We did a lot of sharing.*

*Throughout the day we drew posters that represented certain meditation topics. 'Friendship with God' was one of the banners we had to draw an image for. There was two groups and on the posters or banners we really was competing. It was good fellowshipping, I felt a strong connection of brotherhood.*

*Each group had to make a get-well card for one of the laymen – free-world men – who was in hospital. We drew a cross, some prayer hands in the middle of a heart, and we added a few dove birds.*

*There was a layman there named Jim, another Jim! I put a circle over his head in the photo I'm sending with this letter. He reminded me of you, I told him about you. In the picture it looks like I'm upset but it's just I wasn't ready when it was snapped.*

*This was my second time out there with this group. I enjoyed it more this time. Every guy out there I got to know. The black guy next to Jim is from Nigeria. I talked with him a lot. The way I saw Nigeria was different. He told me I'd been watching too much TV, it's not like that all over his country.*

*Michael isn't doing too fine, he didn't want me to tell you. He's finding it difficult to shake this illness. He's been in and out of the hospital for the last month or so. I talked to him the other day, he'd just got out of the hospital but he fell down and fainted. I don't know what I can do.*

*Yesterday I was glad to get back out to basketball. I'd been eating so good at the retreat I picked up some weight. Before the retreat I got weighed, 207lbs, then Saturday night, two days after I'd attended the retreat, I was 213lbs! That's good eating. The food they had was free-world food, home-cooked food. They fed us twice a day and we was able to get seconds, which I did, and in between they fed us home-baked cookies of all sorts that their wives and fellow members on the outside cooked. The food was prepared with love.*

*There was a few of the laymen that had that shake in their hands that you were talking about and that has you ordering too many books! The guy in the lower left hand corner of the picture got up to speak and he drew out his time line of life on the board and his hand was shaking. He stopped writing and said if you have a problem with my hand shaking I'm sorry, I'm almost eighty years old, this comes with age. I thought of you and your shake. In high school he said that the local town paper reported that he was a promising star running back, a position of offense on a football team, that's very fast and shifty with quickness. I was amazed how he still remembered the newspaper comments from his childhood.*

*I laughed very hard at the picture of the tractor Cathal drew for me. I wouldn't never have guessed that's what it was. He likes tractors, huh? I hope he gets better or else he'll have to find another hobby other than drawing!*

*They did try to kill someone last month but it got held up until further notice by the Supreme Court decision concerning the method of execution. The poison they're using isn't humane enough, they say, as if the act itself is. It looks as if there'll be a nationwide halt to executions until after the US Supreme Court makes a ruling on a case they took from Kentucky. I hope something good comes of this, besides merely changing the drugs they use. As you stated, it's evil regardless how or what method of drugs they use.*

In the death-penalty debate, Native Americans are almost forgotten. In 2006, thirty-nine Native American prisoners, or 1.1 percent of the death-row population, were on death row in seven states in the US. Since 1961, fifteen Native Americans have been executed, thirteen for killing whites and two for killing other Native Americans. Between 1979 and 1999, whites killed 32 percent of the 2,469 Indians murdered, whereas Native Americans killed 1 percent of the 164,377 whites murdered.

The first legally sanctioned execution of a Native American occurred in 1639. Military authorities beheaded Nepauduck for the murder of Abraham Finch, a white man. In 1711, the first recorded execution of a Native American woman occurred when Waisoiusksquaw was hung in Connecticut for the murder of her husband. While thousands of extra-judicial lynchings of Native Americans occurred in American history, 464 Native Americans have been legally executed.

On average Native Americans receive longer sentences and they also tend to serve longer time in prison for their sentences than non-Native Americans. The suicide rate is higher among Native American prisoners and within the prison system they are often subject to abuse when attempting to identify with their own culture through the wearing of headbands, using their own languages, listening to their own music and trying to obtain culturally appropriate educational material.

* * *

In the case of *Baze* v. *Rees*, the US Supreme Court began hearing constitutional challenges to the three-chemical lethal injection used to carry out the death penalty. The case was before the Kentucky Supreme Court in 2004 and came before the US Supreme Court in 2007. It was brought by Ralph Baze and Thomas C. Bowling, two Kentucky death-row inmates who were sentenced to death in 1992 and 1990 respectively for two double murders. Neither faces an imminent execution date. Their appeal claims that the particular drug protocol causes unnecessary pain and suffering that could be avoided, and thus violates the Eighth Amendment ban on ‘cruel and unusual punishment’. John D. Rees is the commissioner of the Kentucky Department of Corrections.

The Berkeley Law Death Penalty Clinic says that the case 'does not attack lethal injection as a method of execution, nor does it challenge the death penalty as a punishment. Rather, it challenges the constitutionality of Kentucky's protocol for administering lethal injection and seeks to ensure that executions by lethal injection are carried out in a manner that complies with the requirements of the Eighth Amendment to avoid cruel and unusual punishment'. Moreover, Baze does not seek a permanent stay of execution. Rather, his defence seeks an injunction preventing the State from executing Baze and Bowling pursuant to a protocol that creates an unnecessary risk of severe pain. If Baze and Bowling win, the State would still be permitted to carry out executions by replacing the current lethal-injection procedure with one that satisfies the standard set by the Supreme Court.

The US Solicitor General, Paul D. Clement, on the other hand, warned the Court that this case may draw it into an unending series of constitutional challenges demanding the use of more humane methods as they come along. The Solicitor General argues that states should not be required to adopt the best available method, the one that causes the least amount of pain when compared to others. He contends that 'there must be some feasible method by which a sentence of death may be executed'; according to the Solicitor General, Kentucky, other states and the federal government have found this in the three-drug protocol.

Pending a decision by the US Supreme Court, a nationwide moratorium on executions came into effect, although as we saw earlier, that moratorium was almost breached by the State of Alabama as it tried to execute James Harvey Callahan in early 2008.

*The first few hours after a visit such as Jim's visit, talking about it and sharing with those that ask questions about it, such as friends and neighbours, is nice. But afterwards it's impossible not to dwell on all that took place and that can be hard, emotionally draining. I usually go to sleep for a while, falling asleep while thinking about all that's taken place.*

*My lawyer was supposed to visit but it's been postponed. They have a scheduled killing next week but it won't go through, the US Supreme Court will stop it as they've done with all the others around the US. Anyway, the prison don't allow visits from lawyers the week of a killing because the family and friends is allowed visit for three or four days before an execution.*

*I got the two books you sent. Thanks. I've started one of them,* Soledad Brother [*sic*]. *I'd already read about George Jackson years ago. I loved how he wouldn't fold to the hands of the oppressors back in the '70s while in prison. Both of these books are accounts of his life in prison, some from letters he'd written. He was killed in prison, shot by the tower guard.*

# 13

## Another Christmas

It is very sad about Michael. Sixty is young these days – it won't help if he thinks he is old and has had enough. . . . Helder Camera, a famous Catholic cardinal in Brazil, I think, said that there are hundreds of definitions of being good – I'm not saying Michael is bad or a sinner – he said it means getting up every time you fall, it doesn't mean never falling. It means being able to say: 'Lord, I have fallen a thousand times. But thanks to you I have got up again a thousand and one times. That's all. I like thinking about that,' said Helder. I have that opinion as a bookmark in my diary. This has nothing to do with Michael, it just came into my mind now and I thought it was a nice story.

No word yet of the book I did in Conamara, although just today I met another Irish-language publisher to whom I had shown some of the manuscript and she said it was very good – realistic, believable, characters good and so on – I was walking on air. For a few minutes! If the publisher I sent the book to accepts it, then he will do everything – deal with printers, distribute to bookshops – and I can just lie back and dream of huge literary prizes, the adulation of fans and beautiful pop stars! Dream on!

Finally, Ray, another nice story! I was reading a book in a bookshop the other day – I sometimes read books in bookshops. The book was about Christy Ring, a native of Cork like me, a great hurling hero, unlike me, really famous, he featured in that piece I wrote about the pyracantha bush. In 1953, a woman in Cork was wheeling her baby girl along the road in her pram when a car tried to overtake a lorry and was speeding towards her and she was terrified it would hit the pram. But the lorry driver saw what was happening and pulled up on the footpath so that the car could pass safely. The woman turned around to thank the lorry driver and immediately recognised Christy. . . . Twenty-five years later, the legendary hurler, Christy Ring, was walking along a street in Cork city when he dropped down stone dead. The first person to come to his assistance was a twenty-five-year old nurse who just happened to be – the baby in the pram. And on that note . . . Slán for a while, Ray.

* * *

*I'm good, taking care of myself, doing the usual, staying out of trouble. Guess what? I'm a hall runner again! I assist the guys on the tier and pass out ice, trays. I come out from 2 to 9 PM, Mondays and Tuesdays, I've been working for a couple of weeks. I've gotten a little freedom back!*

*I knew after you got my letter about Michael, you would understand. But in the event you didn't, I hope you trust in my judgement and don't think of me as a non-compassionate person. I felt you wanted to disregard what I requested of you – to send the $ to Jim so that he would forward it on to me – because you felt like I was being inconsiderate. I would never do something like that to a friend I trust. Honestly I was kinda offended by the fact you was going to overrule my wishes, which you have the right to do, but that don't to me show a lot of trust in my judgement. You must know I know what's best for me in my situation. But trust me, if I didn't think I had to make this change I wouldn't. Michael has been and still is one of the best guys I ever met in my life.*

*I talked to him last night and he told me he went and paid for his funeral and he was dying. Can you imagine having such a conversation with one of your best friends. Of course, I wanted to know how he was so sure and he just stuck with 'he knew it'. And he spoke of how we, you and I, will be on the 'to contact' list. He said he got the $ from you. Thanks. I'm going to get me a pair of shoes, I just completely wore out my other pair on the basketball court last week.*

*Sounds like you did a good job painting the converted attic for Cathal and family! Well, besides bumping your head regularly, you did good. Why didn't you take a page out of Cathal's book and wear your 'Bob the Builder' hard hat! Say hi to everyone and I hope all is well and joyful.*

Cathal is quite calm about Christmas, I don't think he really knows what is going on, he calls Santa 'Ho Ho' (like some Chinese leader!) but he sings Rudolph and the carol 'the little Lord Jesus lay down his sweet head'. He was here for a while today and we put up the decorations on the tree and he put the figures in the crib – 'Jesus, Mary and Jowuff'.

It is very cold at the moment. The city is usually a bit warmer than the country. The water we put out for the birds to drink and bathe in freezes every night. You'd know the weather is cold by the strange birds in the garden at the moment, mainly redwings, field fare and redcaps. They come down from the mountains when the weather gets bad. We had the holly tree covered with netting but when we cut enough for ourselves and the family we took off the netting and the birds are delighted! They are feasting on the holly berries and the pyracantha berries at the end of the garden.

Tomorrow is the shortest day of the year here and after that the days will be getting longer. A couple of days ago I tidied up the garden – weeds, leaves etc – and noticed that daffodils, despite the cold, are peeking up above the ground already. Normally they flower end of February or March. We were at a Traveller wedding a couple of weeks ago – did I tell you about it? – and the bridesmaids wore dresses the colour of daffodils – I had never seen bridesmaids wearing that colour before but they really lit up the place.

*I've been enjoying my holidays for the most part. We got our Xmas packages and that certainly brought some form of joy around for us all. I'm enclosing my copy of the items so you can see what I got and am eating on and will be eating on for at least another month. These packages come in handy, they allow me to pass up most of those untasty trays the prison serves us. That's really the only thing that's different and worth talking about that takes place in the prison. I didn't get no visit from the family, my sisters had to work so my mom said it'll be after Christmas.*

*Thanks for the pictures you sent. The one of you in the garden digging up bulbs – it looks like you've been eating good, I can see you have put on a few pounds since the last picture I have of you. There's nothing wrong with that. You told me on many occasions how good Aunt Bríd's cooking is, so it's not your fault! You say you're 216lbs, you outweigh me by six or seven pounds but that'll more than likely change after I've eaten up all my package food.*

*Yeah, the faith-group people come around about once a month, four or five come and walk around the tiers and fellowship with the guys that want to talk. They split up and walk around death row.*

*About Michael, that's nothing, it's all good, 'no sweat' as I would say around here. I understand, as I hope you do, that I'm one of the most loyal people you'll ever meet when it comes to my friends and loved ones. Desert them or leave them hanging in a time of need isn't my style, never has been. When I make choices it's for the better of all involved. I've never been selfish or uncompassionate and not to have Michael's best interests at heart I would be both of those things. Every intention of mine is to help him and let him know he's not alone. He is lonely. I have a lot of experience in being judged and being an outcast in my life. And we, Michael and I, connected on that level and built a family-type bond.*

*Anyway, again don't you feel bad about suggesting I shouldn't get somebody else to do the things Michael had been doing for me. I didn't take what you said to heart but I won't lie, I felt like you didn't know me as well as I thought you did, but that reflects back on me also for not making it clearer to you the way things are. So I don't or didn't take it to heart.*

*You remember the quote from Helder Camera that you sent to me as a bookmark? Where he says it's not how many times we fall, but how many times we get up. That's a good quote to have on a bookmark, to constantly be reminded of that is nice. Would it be possible to send one of those bookmarks?*

* * *

*Grace sent me two pictures of Conamara, west coast of Ireland, they are some beautiful pictures, the view is so amazing. Looking at them I thought I could smell the air. If I'm ever in Ireland, somebody must take me to Cork and Conamara for sure. On the pictures it's nothing but water across to the next mountain, or rather island. I would just like to stand in the middle of the green field or atop the bank and just scream as loud as I can and converse with the skies about whatever comes to mind at the time! Do that sound crazy? I'm going to enclose these two pics, send them back, but I've got to share them. . . . I just thought – remember how I didn't like those country and rural settings and the peace of them all? Now I'm seeing the delight in it. Could that be because I'm getting old?!*

*The hall-running job is going fine and yes, it certainly will build up the legs, going up and down the stairs, but it also is wearing on them! After a shift my legs and feet are tired. You said to me to remember that the customer is always right. Yes, I would imagine so in McDonald's, not in prison though!*

You said that you noticed from the photos, Ray, that I've put on a few pounds. I was very 'hurt' by your comments about my weight! I'll have you know I lost about 6lb and look slightly thinner. If you look closely! I'm back walking and get in a walk almost every day.

Not to worry. The other day Eoin patted my stomach and gave as his learned opinion that it was 'too small for twins'!

*So you liked the bridesmaids' dresses at the wedding of Andy and Mary and their bright daffodil yellow colour. Now you can't say you've never seen bridesmaids light up a wedding! Travellers sound to have an interesting life, very different from the standards set by society. I don't think you did anything wrong in saying to Mary that she'll miss her mum and dad after she's married and moved sixty miles away. It was certainly the truth, one she'll have to realise one way or the other. . . . I'm more in agreement with you. Mary could've kept on at school and thought of settling down with marriage when that was over. And her young cousin that's only fifteen and engaged to be married. Why do they start so young to live an adult life with marriage and all? That's strange to me. I think at fifteen years old you should be out playing with girls, not picking wedding dresses out.*

*No, the articles you sent about the death penalty didn't upset me. They were factual and true. A lot of the facts about the US I was already aware of. We too feel like this legal murdering is about to come to an end, sooner or later. It's very inspiring to see the numbers declining around the US and not just in one State. I'd like to be always optimistic about it but it's hard, this being the US. But who knows . . . if there's enough supporters for us, I do think that eventually they will have to do away with capital punishment throughout the country. We just got to outlive it until it happens. . . .*

*Have you got the car troubles sorted out, I hope so. The thought of you all stranded on the roadside for three hours like you spoke of, wasn't nice. My mother had car trouble also over Christmas – one of the reasons I didn't get a visit.*

*Also – a belated happy birthday! I've always been told the older you get the more you'd rather not celebrate. Is this true? Did you celebrate? Or get gifts? And if so, what?*

*I haven't talked to Rachel in a while. My sister don't live near her anymore, she was evicted, did I tell you that? Anyway, she was and that's where I used to talk to Rachel. It's hard now so I write a lot or send cards. My father, I haven't heard or talked to him in many many months. I sent him a card and a copy of some photos but I don't even know if he got them. As the years pass I have less and less contact with my people I left behind. It's just how it is with some folks. Sad but true.*

On 17 December 2007, Democratic Governor Jon Corzine, a long-time opponent of the death penalty, made New Jersey the first state in the modern era of capital punishment to repeal by legislation its death penalty. Corzine signed a bill that had been fast-tracked through the legislature. In the previous two weeks, the bill was passed in both the Senate and the Assembly with the narrowest of majorities after impassioned floor debates. New Jersey has not executed anyone in forty-four years.

A statewide poll taken earlier in 2007 showed that by a margin of 51 percent to 41 percent, the people of New Jersey preferred that criminals be sentenced to life in prison without parole instead of death.

The State Senate president, Richard Codey, a Republican, said he had voted for the current law in 1982 because it provided for 'exhaustive appeals' to make sure that those convicted were definitely guilty. Since then, prosecutors have won sixty death sentences, but fifty-two have been reversed and there have been no executions. 'How can I argue the deterrent effect of the death penalty when we haven't had one?' Mr Codey asked.

In late November, family members of sixty-two murder victims sent a letter to legislators urging passage of the abolition Bill. The relatives emphasised the personal toll the process had taken on them. 'Capital punishment drags victims' loved ones through an agonising and lengthy process, holding out the promise of one punishment in the beginning and often resulting in a life sentence in the end anyway,' the letter said.

A group of police chiefs and prosecutors said in late November that 'despite our very best intentions, the system makes mistakes and innocent people are wrongfully sentenced to death'. In May 2007, a New Jersey prisoner was exonerated by DNA testing after he had spent seventeen years on death row.

The Sant'Egidio Community, the lay Roman Catholic organisation which is at the forefront of the international anti-death penalty movement, praised the New Jersey decision, saying it is a 'crucial passage' for a worldwide moratorium on capital punishment. The Community said that Rome's Colosseum would be lit up when Governor Corzine signed the legislation abolishing the death penalty. (The Colosseum, once the arena for deadly gladiatorial combat and executions, has become a symbol of the fight against capital punishment. Since 1999, the monument has been bathed in golden light every time a death sentence is commuted somewhere in the world or every time a country abolishes capital punishment.)

There were further hopeful signs as 2007 came to an end. The UN General Assembly adopted a resolution calling for a moratorium on the death penalty, despite opposition from the US, China and others, who argued that each country should be able to choose how to combat crime. The 104–54 vote for suspending executions is not legally binding. There were twenty-nine abstentions. 'There is no conclusive evidence of the death penalty's deterrence value and any miscarriage or failure of justice in the death penalty's implementation is irreversible and irreparable,' the proposers of the resolution said.

Attempts in 1994 and 1999 to have the assembly adopt a moratorium on the death penalty failed. But since then, the number of countries that have abolished capital punishment in law or practice has grown to 133, according to Amnesty International.

'Today's vote represents a bold step by the international community,' UN Secretary General Ban Ki-moon said. 'This is further evidence of a trend towards ultimately abolishing the death penalty.' When Ban came into office at the beginning of 2007, he responded to questions about the execution of Saddam Hussein by saying that each country should be allowed to choose its own policies, but he quickly embraced the official UN anti-death penalty view. The EU, which requires its members to outlaw capital punishment, led the UN campaign. Italy's foreign minister, Massimo D'Alema, came to New York for the vote and hailed it as 'an important step'. The Colosseum was illuminated to celebrate the moratorium resolution.

The United States joined China, Iran, Sudan and Syria in opposing the resolution, arguing that it interfered with their sovereign rights. 'Capital punishment remains legal under international law and Barbados wishes to exercise its sovereign right to use it as a deterrent to the most serious crimes,' said the delegate from Barbados before the vote.

According to Amnesty International, China is the world leader in executions. China, Iran, Iraq, Pakistan, Sudan and the US account for 91 percent of all capital punishment. Forty-two people were executed in the US in 2007, the lowest number since 1994 and less than half the figure for 1999. That year, the US total was ninety-eight, the highest in the modern era of the death penalty. Only ten states held executions in 2007, and twenty-six executions occurred in one state: Texas. In China, where state executions are carried out in secret, Amnesty said that it had established that in 2007 at least 470 people were executed (nine a week) and a further 1,860 (thirty-five a week) were sentenced to death. About 27,500 people were on death row globally in 2007. Second to China in number of executions was Iran (317), followed by Saudi Arabia (143), Pakistan (135) and the US (42). Between them, these five countries accounted for 88 percent of all known executions.

One of the main arguments against the death penalty is the random and arbitrary way in which it works. Each year, less than 2 percent (about 280 people) of the 14,000 people who commit murder are selected to die.

The death penalty is not necessarily applied to the worst of the worst offenders: in 2004, Charles Cullen, a former nurse, escaped the death penalty in an agreement with prosecutors in which he pleaded guilty to killing thirteen hospital patients. In 2003, Gary Ridgway, who had admitted to forty-eight murders since 1982, was sentenced to life without parole. Washington state prosecutors spared Ridgway from execution in exchange for his cooperation in leading police to the remains of missing victims.

The courts may be arbitrary when it comes to imposing the death penalty. In April 2007, the *Cincinnati Enquirer* pointed out that the voting record of judges in the US Court of Appeals is extremely mixed:

| *President making appointments* | *% of votes by judges against defendants* | *% of votes for defendants* |
|---|---|---|
| Jimmy Carter | 11 | 89 |
| Ronald Reagan | 75 | 25 |
| George H. W. Bush | 93 | 7 |
| Bill Clinton | 30 | 70 |
| George W. Bush | 87 | 13 |

Whether a person receives the death penalty or not depends heavily on where the crime was committed. Neighbouring states in the same region can have different practices. For instance, Iowa does not practise the death penalty, while Missouri does; Massachusetts does not practise the death penalty, but Connecticut does. In this unfair system, the simple act of crossing state lines can be the difference between life and death.

There are also disparities within states. In New York, although upstate counties experience 19 percent of the state's homicides, they account for 61 percent of all capital prosecutions. In Indiana, a 2001 investigation by seven state newspapers found that two Indiana counties have produced almost as many death sentences as all of the other Indiana counties combined. The same investigation found that willingness to seek the death penalty also depended on factors such as the views of individual prosecutors and the ability of a county to meet the enormous cost of capital punishment.

In 2003, the Capital Jury Project studied more than 1,200 jurors from fourteen states and concluded that the guidelines for jurors and for the elimination of arbitrary sentencing were not working. Interviews with jurors found that approximately 50 percent of those interviewed decided what the penalty should be before the sentencing phase of the trial. Researchers found that jury-selection methods resulted in guilty verdicts being returned and death sentences being handed down in a disproportionate number of cases. The study found that 45 percent of jurors failed to understand that they were allowed to consider any mitigating evidence during the sentencing phase of the trial and that two-thirds of jurors failed to realise that unanimity was not required for findings of mitigation.

The research also revealed that the chances of a death sentence being handed down in cases with a black defendant and white victim increase when there are five or more white males on the jury, and the chances decrease when there is at least one black male on the jury. These two groups of jurors have very different perspectives regarding lingering doubt, and the remorsefulness of, and future danger posed by, defendants.

Early findings of the study found that most jurors grossly underestimated the amount of time a defendant would serve in prison if he or she was not sentenced to death, and that the sooner jurors believed a defendant would return to society if not given the death penalty, the more likely they were to vote for death.

States vary greatly in the quality of representation they provide to indigent defendants, and this contributes to mistakes in capital sentencing. In 1990, a prominent law journal described capital trials as being 'more like a random flip of the coin than a delicate balancing of scales', because the defence attorneys were often badly trained and unprepared. In Washington state, one-fifth of the eighty-four people who faced execution (in the period 1981 to 2000) were represented by lawyers who have been disbarred, suspended or arrested. In North Carolina, at least sixteen death-row inmates, including three who were subsequently executed, were represented by lawyers who had been disbarred or disciplined for unethical or criminal conduct. In Texas, about one in four death-row inmates have been defended by lawyers who have been reprimanded, placed on probation, suspended or banned from practising law by the State Bar (*Dallas Morning News*, 2000). The *New York Times* reported that in Alabama in 2001 about 40 of the approximately 185 inmates who were then on death row did not have counsel.

The US Supreme Court (*Furman v Georgia*) has said that if the death penalty is applied arbitrarily, it should not be applied at all.

The Court ruled that punishment randomly applied is cruel punishment and, for that very reason, it struck down the death penalty in 1972. Opponents of the death penalty believe that, since the reinstatement of the death penalty in 1976, the criminal-justice system is still arbitrary and random.

*Thanks for all the photos. You've changed your occupation from painter to photographer, huh? The one of Cathal and Bríd putting up the Christmas decorations was a nice picture and Cathal thinking he's a genius for being able to go up the small ladder! From the picture of the dry-stone walls around Catherine and Martin's house it's obvious that things have come a long way since the last picture I saw of the house. The wall and the willow gate look good and I agree the letter box is crooked but as long as it opens and closes, I suppose it could be all right?*

*Róisín, in the picture with Aunt Bríd and Francis at the holy well, looks like a little lady. A Little Miss Sunshine, she's posing for the pic and sipping her water like she know what she's doing! And Cathal is looking at Liam as if they've not only been having a good time but like they were having a good one while the pic was being taken. I guess I would've been just as gleeful if I was Cathal's age at a table full of loved ones – and sweets! I see cookies and cake!*

*Thanks for the article you got off* Counterpunch. *I don't know much about politics or this lady but I must admit from what I've heard Benazir Bhutto was very courageous. I do think from the way they said she acted after she came out of exile, that she wanted to be a martyr and wasn't fearful of death. I saw on the world news the attempt on her life, the first day she returned out of exile. If that was me that would be all the proof I needed that I wasn't welcome back but for some odd reason she was under the impression they wouldn't kill her because she was a woman. What are your thoughts of her and all of this? I also think she was manipulated out of exile by the USA and they dropped the ball in protecting her. If she was so valued she would have been protected far better than she was. Do you think that would have happened to Bush or Condoleeza Rice if they were over there?*

*Catherine will have got back to work by the time you get this. How's that worked out for her? I'm sure she missed her kids and they missed her. I'd say you were on to something when you said politicians don't care about therapy for disabled children with 26,000 children on the waiting lists and 1,200 unfilled jobs for therapists.*

*You spoke of there being racist chants, e.g. when black players are on the ball and so on. What did you mean by that? Chants such as what? Do that not cause trouble in the crowds?*

We are all well here. 'A quiet Christmas' – but everybody says that when you ask them what kind of Christmas they had. They say Christmas was generally quiet in Ireland – shops quieter than other years, more people staying at home, probably because the Guards were out in force breathalysing people; accidents were down too. The weather is very cold – it is often like that here after Christmas – but soon the days will be getting longer.

We went on a short post-Christmas visit to County Clare. We just missed seeing a calf being born. When we got there he still could not stand. The cow was licking him all over to clean him, it's amazing they know what to do without being taught! The farmer, Micheál, lives just beside Catherine and Martin and was very helpful to them when they were settling in. He has a closed-circuit TV in the barn so that he can keep an eye on things and he can stay at home by the fire and he doesn't have to go down to the barn until things are at the critical stage. But in this case he hadn't to do anything, the cow knew it all!

Liam is well. There was a big fire in north London on Saturday night but it was far enough away from him. It was in Camden, which has become part of the social scene, with pubs and clubs, and also has very expensive property, including a two-bedroom apartment for £1.2 million! Forty to fifty years ago people who emigrated from Ireland often lived in poor accommodation in Camden town and used stand at the street corners in the morning waiting for building contractors to come along in their vans to offer them work. It was a very hard life but things have improved for the Irish and now it's Asians who wait at the corners.

The racist chants happen when a black player gets the ball and then some of the supporters of the opposing team start making monkey sounds, shouting about bananas. One car-racing driver was verbally abused a few weeks ago by a group who dressed up like golliwogs and started chanting at him. That was in Spain, and I see in the paper today that he was racing in China yesterday and got the same treatment. Liam was at a soccer match in London and he said the chants were unprintable, so I can't write them down here!

Did I tell you that Goretti, our friend from Zimbabwe, has gone to work with the UN in Liberia, west Africa, for three months. We hadn't heard from her and then she sent us this e-mail:

> I'm OK emotionally but keep missing home and the family. I met Pakistani soldiers who are deployed here, they were most welcoming and warm. It was my first time to deal with Pakistani people at such a level, they are very very hospitable and helpful. The senior soldier, a Major, I think, offered to have the Pakistani engineers refurbish a small cosy aprtment for me, it's really not bad. I'm the first professional woman to be posted to this place, so it's quite a challenge . . .
>
> I am fine, trying to be strong. The roads here are damaged or they are dusty roads which are hard and sometimes even inaccessible in rainy season. It is summer now until April when it starts raining until December, and I'm told it's heavy rains. Anyway we drive 4x4 Nissan Patrol jeeps which are big and powerful, so that they can

deal with the terrain. I'm actually going to do an all-terrain driving course this coming week. The streets in the capital, Monrovia, are very crowded and the driving is awful, people ignore traffic rules all the time.

I am going to a village called Bopulu and will be team leader for the county called Gbarpolu which has six districts. It is situated in north-western Liberia, it covers an area of 1,263 sq miles with a population of 131,227 (1984 census), it is one of the hottest biodiversity spots in Liberia and has significant resources and wildlife.

The place I'm going to is a little village. (They insist on calling it a city). There is significant poverty, most of the houses are pole and dagga [wattle and daub] houses, no electricity and running water. There are no shops for basic food supplies and groceries, there are small shops which the locals can use. I stock up in Monrovia and the distance to Bopulu is 54 km, dust road, which took me about two hours to drive. For those used to driving on these roads, it takes about one hour. The good news is that a new road will be opened by the end of February, and will link up Monrovia and Bopulu.

Fortunately my accommodation will have electricity twenty-four hours, running water and air-conditioning. The office has air conditioning also, it's only when I'm working outside that I will feel the heat. The roads are dusty, I can't wear my high heels and some of my clothes! I have to be practical.

The soil is very fertile, but there's little farming going on, partly because of inaccessible roads. Three of the six districts in the county are accessible by car, the others are not and the only mode of transport is to walk.

Some human-rights issues are treatment of detained persons: the government of Liberia does not provide them with food, instead it asks the victims of crime to bring food for the accused. There is food insecurtiy, poor health facilities, poor education facilities, no teachers, sexual and domestic violence. My job will be monitoring these practices, providing training for police and other government officials about implementing human rights, promoting human rights through school human rights clubs and other creative ways. Anyway this info should keep you going . . . today is Saturday and is a working day up to 2 PM. I'm in Monrovia, I might join a group of international UN staff and local people and go on a hash. This is where a different location is chosen each week and some go running, i.e. those who can, and some walk. I will be walking, it's a way of seeing different places. . . .

* * *

*You sound like you've become attached to your pullover sweater, at least in the winter time. And if you've had it six years and it's still like new, I can understand why Donegal is famous for its knitted and tweed stuff.*

*It seems like everyone is having car trouble, here and there. You know I notice every time something go wrong with a car, it's always more than the original problem you think it is. Why's that? My mom's radiator first and then the water pump. Your clutch and then the timing belt in the VW, and then the clutch and the drive shaft in the Mazda.*

*I smiled at what you said about my comment that I would love to shout and scream at the sky from the middle of the fields – near the Sky Road, you think. You said: 'Whatever slight touch of craziness there might be involved in that would be entirely understandable!' I also liked what you said about my wanting to get to places like Cork and Conamara – it isn't a sign of getting old but a sign that my judgment is improving! Thanks!*

# 14

# As Befits a Man

On 8 February 2008, Nebraska's Supreme Court ruled that execution using the electric chair violated the state's constitution and was a cruel and unusual punishment. This brought executions of this type to an end in Nebraska. The state's death penalty remains on the statute books, but the court said that the legislature must approve another method of execution if it wishes to implement the death penalty. 'We recognise the temptation to make the prisoner suffer, just as the prisoner made an innocent victim suffer. But it is the hallmark of a civilized society that we punish cruelty without practicing it,' the court's majority wrote in its 6–1 decision. Nebraska was the only state that still used the electric chair as its sole means of execution. The penalty was challenged by lawyers for Raymond Mata Jr, who was sentenced to death for killing a three-year-old boy. The evidence shows that electrocution inflicts 'intense pain and agonizing suffering,' the court said. In 2007, the State changed its method to one twenty-second jolt of 2,450 volts, instead of four shorter shocks.

The electric chair was first used for an execution in 1890. It was used by more than twenty-five states throughout the twentieth century, along the way picking up nicknames such as 'Sizzlin' Sally', 'Old Smokey', 'Old Sparky', 'Yellow Mama' and 'Gruesome Gertie'. In the 1880s, electricity was a new and novel power source. When New York State introduced the electric chair, it was claimed that it would provide a more humane method of execution. Not so.

Alabama, April 1983: the execution of John Evans. After the first jolt of electricity, sparks and flames erupted from the electrode attached to Evans's leg. The electrode then burst from the strap holding it in place and caught fire. Smoke and sparks came out from under the hood. Two doctors entered the chamber and found a heartbeat. The electrode was re-attached. More smoke and burning flesh. Again doctors found a heartbeat. Ignoring the pleas of Evans's lawyer, a third jolt was applied. The execution took fourteen minutes and left Evans's body charred and smouldering.

In December 1984, the state of Georgia electrocuted Alpha Otis Stephens. After the first jolt of electricity failed to kill him, Stephens struggled for eight minutes before a second charge finished the job. The first jolt lasted two minutes, and there was a six-minute pause to allow his body to cool sufficiently for doctors to examine him. He was still breathing and the doctors declared that another jolt was needed. In May 1990, Jesse Joseph Tafero, husband of Sunny Jacobs, was electrocuted in Florida. When the state replaced a 'natural' sponge with a synthetic sponge in the headpiece of the execution apparatus, six-inch flames erupted, and three jolts of power were required to stop Tafero's breathing.

In July 1999, again in Florida, when Allen Lee Davis was hit with 2,300 volts, blood poured from his mouth. The blood poured on to the collar of his white shirt, and oozed on to his chest. By the time he was pronounced dead, the stain on Davis's chest had grown to the size of a dinner plate, and the blood had seeped through buckle holes on the leather chest strap holding him to the chair. Davis was the first inmate to be executed in Florida's new electric chair. Details of other appallingly gruesome examples of botched executions can be read on *www.ccadp.org/botchedx.htm.*

In the late twentieth century, the electric chair was removed as a form of execution in many US states, in favour of the lethal-injection method. More than 150 people have been executed by electrocution since the death penalty was reinstated in 1976.

I hope you got the photo which I sent to you as a postcard – I never did that before. A few miles from where Catherine lives, a farmer has a herd of cattle called 'belted Galloways'. They are a Scottish breed. I never saw them before. They are strange to look at. All around their bellies a big belt of their hide is pure white. Looks peculiar! And they don't seem to be a bit embarrassed by it!

Goretti sent another e-mail. This one was sent after her return from Ghana, after six weeks the UN volunteers got a weekend rest break in Ghana:

> I'm fine. Ghana was really good, I enjoyed it and was able to de-stress. I visited a lot of places there, including the dungeons where slaves were kept. It was heart-rending being in those places, I broke down and cried when the torture that they went through was narrated. When I saw the dark tunnels they lived in, no air or sunlight, when I saw the torture equipment, and the door of no return where the slaves went through, it was just too much, and can you imagine there was a church where the Europeans prayed on top of the dungeons. That's too sad, eh?
>
> Work is still enjoyable. I am running a human-rights poster competition for schools and have picked up the entries, really fascinating stuff. I'm also helping with the Truth and Reconciliation Commission, working on domestic violence and peace-building. I'm also monitoring prisons, courts, police stations.
>
> Today this old lady whom I have befriended gave me a live chicken to take home. I was so touched, and by the way a group of women have given me a new name, Hawa, because mine was difficult to pronounce. So much to say. I will be coming home end of the month and I'm excited about it . . . but it will be with a heavy heart that I will leave this place.

We saw a good documentary on TV about San Quentin Prison. It only dealt with the general population, some people had very long sentences. What struck me was the noise – always noise. We saw some 'single walk' cages and heard prisoners talking about being intimidated by others. It was a kind of chilling programme. I think I told you that when we were in San Francisco once, we drove out past San Quentin. A huge yellow monster of a building.

My birthday was quiet but nice, cake with grandchildren, some of them. Got useful presents – shirt, tie, socks! But sure I don't really need anything. The two cars are fixed and going well – I must remember to take my foot off the clutch at all times. Automatics are few and far between in Ireland.

That well, the holy one which specialises in cures for diabetes? Well, it doesn't work! My blood-sugar count is on the up, not dangerous or anything like that. I think any kind of excitement, Christmas or new baby, puts it up.

Is your Mom's visit to you going ahead? And I was very sorry to hear your sister's accommodation problems. Where does she stay now? Is it hard to get public housing? There is an economic downturn here, especially in construction, hundreds of jobs being lost, no cranes on the skyline any more.

You are not finished reading yet, Ray! Below is an e-mail I got from my friend Benny, who is in the US at the moment. I think I told you that he was taking a year out in America, I don't know how he manages it. I told you too about the girl I met with him, it's unclear if she is still around although he does mention 'we'! This e-mail comes from Redwoods Monastery in California: Benny spent the new year there. I've put some explanations/clarifications in brackets. Here goes:

> This year my roommate of last New Year is not here at Redwoods Monastery, but then he is a recidivist. So he celebrates Christmas and the New Year in a penitentiary. At the age of seventy-five he still hasn't learnt the lesson of Empire. But Louis is a Franciscan (like I was once, remember OFM?) and a priest, he was even a superior of the Franciscan Order at one stage, and he takes his faith seriously. He and Steve, a Jesuit, are doing a five-month sentence for protesting at Fort Huachuca in Arizona, where the US military teaches interrogation and torture techniques. Steve is doing the time in solitary confinement as he refuses to do prison work.

It is good to be back here. On the two-day journey up Highway 101 to get here, we remembered what Ladon, a member of the Los Angeles Catholic Worker (the people who damaged the US warplane in Shannon, belonged to the Catholic Worker Movement), used to say: 'You become that with which you habitually associate.' He too took his faith seriously, leaving behind a position as vice president of Xerox, an apartment in Manhattan, and land in the South to divide his time between a Trappist (monks, contemplative, little talk, lots of work and prayer) monastery in the mountains, the soup kitchen in LA that serves the homeless on skid row, and long periods of incarceration for his witness in the face of the military-industrial complex.

In Redwood City we conversed with Larry, who had been a priest; many involved with the Catholic Worker Movement were previously religious. We explored the suggestion that the Cross implies the intersection of personal choices taken at great personal cost in the face of societal values. Good conversations – food for body, soul and spirit!

Here in this Trappist monastery of eleven monks, ten women and one man, a sense of celebrating the advent of a new year in community has evolved. Folk gather from different parts to reflect on the year which has passed, to remember and be re-remembered by the experiences it has held, and to anticipate the year which dawns and become conscious of the hopes one holds for the next stage of one's journey. It is a place in which Thomas Merton from Gethsemani in Kentucky spent time.

The setting is in the middle of the great redwoods. Here deer wander close to the cabins where we stay, in the river there are salmon that have travelled eighty miles upstream from the ocean to spawn. Here there is a sense of things being in order in the natural world.

I tell my friend, Tom, who is seven, the story – which all Irish children know – of Fionn and the Salmon of Knowledge before we go to a pool where the salmon sometimes rest on their journey. When we get there I have a big job holding him back in his desire to become a warrior.

Jim from Toronto is spending a couple of months here. He spent time here before heading to Iraq with Christian Peacemaker Teams a couple of years back. It was one of the things which helped him survive the 118 days and nights during which he and his three companions were kept chained to each other before one of them, Tom Fox, was taken away and executed.

On my last night we talk a little about his experience over dinner when the usual silence is relaxed. One of the significant things for him was that he never allowed his dignity to be taken away. Interestingly, his experience suggested to him that absolute powerlessness corrupts every bit as much as absolute power.

I talk with Veronique, who was one of the original group of monks to come from Belgium in 1962 to establish the monastery, about life, about the world, and about some writing I might explore. 'You will write', she insists! She talks about the struggle between light and dark, how we all experience it in our daily lives but maybe not as extreme as in the bigger scenarios. She talks of the power of goodness, how we all are seeking this, we all have had this but 'things have gone wrong'.

At vespers (prayers monks chant at evening time) the prayer becomes 'What do You call me to?' I remember a conversation with a friend Sybille in Berlin a couple of months back when she talked of cultivation and culture. What is the culture we need to surround ourselves with in order to become who we are uniquely called to be? Sometimes the right question is much more important than the answer.

## And this, Ray, is the story of Fionn and the Salmon of Knowledge which Benny mentioned:

'Truth in our hearts, strength in our limbs and deeds according to our words' was the motto of the Fianna, the noble warriors who lived in Ireland long ago. It is said that no man could join the Fianna until he could pass the following tests. He had to be able to:

- § Recite the twelve books of poetry which told of the great deeds of the heroes of ancient Ireland;
- § Defend himself against the spears of nine warriors;
- § Race through the oak and birch woods of Ireland without breaking a twig;

- § Leap over a standing spear the height of himself;
- § Pass under a stick as low as his knee;
- § Remove a thorn from his foot while running.

The great leader of the Fianna was called Cumhall. His son Fionn was only a small child when the men of Clan Mórna killed Cumhall in battle. His mother was afraid that Clan Mórna would try to kill Fionn too. She asked two wise women to hide him in a safe place and care for him.

The wise women took Fionn to a lonely valley deep in the woods on Slieve Bloom in the centre of Ireland. The young boy learned from them many of the stories of the great heroes. Not only did they fill his mind with wondrous lore and tales, they also took care of his physical education. They taught him to swim by throwing him into a deep pool in the Nore river and leaving him to make his own way out! To train him to run quickly, they made him herd hares in a field with no fence or hedge! Fionn grew up straight and tall. At last the day came for him to leave the lonely valley in Slieve Bloom and the wise women and go to one of the wise druids called Finnéigeas to learn the ancient art of poetry.

Finnéigeas lived beside the River Boyne in Cúige na Mí. He had chosen that place because it was always beside flowing river water that poetry was revealed to him.

Near to his cabin grew the nine hazel trees of knowledge. Their branches overhung a deep pool in the River Boyne. Nuts of wisdom fell from these trees into the pool and in that pool lived the salmon of knowledge. The ancient druids had foretold that whoever first ate of this salmon would possess all the wisdom in the world. Finnéigeas had fished for many long years, but had failed to catch the salmon of knowledge.

A short time after Fionn came to him, he fished for the salmon and succeeded in catching it. Finnéigeas was delighted. He instructed Fionn to cook the salmon but not to eat any of it. Fionn cooked the salmon with care, turning it over and over. When it was ready, he served it to his master.

Finnéigeas saw that Fionn was changed. In his eyes shone the light of wisdom.

'Tell me boy, have you eaten any of this salmon?' he asked.

'No, master, I have not, but as I was cooking the salmon a blister rose on its skin and when I tried to smooth it down I burnt my thumb. I put my thumb in my mouth to ease the pain.'

Finnéigeas knew then that Fionn had received the wisdom of the salmon.

'Here, take the salmon of knowledge and eat it since you have tasted it first,' he said, returning the fish to him.

Fionn ate the salmon, and as he did so he became possessed of all the wisdom of the world. From that time, he had only to bite the thumb that he had burned and he could discover the secrets of hidden magic and see into the future.

Fionn soon left Finnéigeas and journeyed to Tara, where he went through many great trials on his way to becoming the leader of the Fianna like his father before him. But that is a story for another day.

And so Slán for another while, Ray. We send you all our best wishes for everything you wish for yourself. Let me know about Michael. We are thinking of him also.

* * *

*The e-mails from Goretti were nice to read, all very culture-shocking to say the least, not that I wasn't somewhat aware of such living there. Getting them first-hand experiences is something I truly cherish and am thankful for. Not in a million years would I ever have thought I would connect and build such a life with such souls outside of the projects in my home town. I actually feel like I'm part of your family. And please know this. I can't fully express my thanks enough. And tell Goretti her strength and will is inspiring to a little thirty-something old black guy on death row.*

*You want to know something I've never told anyone before? My biggest fear of meeting my demise isn't death itself but the thought of being forgotten by those that I care about, and I often think of that. What do you think that says about me, if anything at all?*

*Michael is fine. I haven't heard from him in a week or so. His phone is down so I just write and wait for his replies as they come. I understand and will take heed to what you was saying about pushing him too much in case that has the opposite effect of what's intended. I try to alert him more so to the fact of him being somebody that's needed in this world. I try to let him know he's not alone and is cared for. It's unpleasant to watch him being down when he's withstood all the judgments and other cruel things that come with life.*

*The hall running is going okay. I got to work tomorrow. The customers are happy, or as happy as they're going to get if I got anything to do with it!*

*My sister is now staying with my mom. I got a letter from her a few days ago. She was telling me she's moving into her own place next month and she's looking forward to that, as I'm sure my mom is also. What about the cars? Have you been remembering to take your foot off the clutch? I can't even drive stick shifts, or rather I can but the clutch certainly won't last long, so I suppose that means I can't, right? Why is it automatics are few over there?*

*P.S. How do you know those belted galloways wasn't embarrassed? Maybe they was!*

Hi, Ray. You talk about the fear of being forgotten. I suppose a time will come when nobody on earth either knows or remembers you but I think that is a good bit away. I think I told you about getting my father's full birth certificate with the name of his parents on it.We now know his father's name and his mother's name. We never knew that before but now we will always remember and never forget their names. The same with you, Ray, you will always be remembered in some way or other and especially by those you love, and they will pass on from generation to generation the stories about you. All our children will tell their children about you and Eoin, and Róisín, Cathal and Séamus will know you and recognise you when they see you in a photo album here. Though you and I will eventually be forgotten, it won't be for a while – about 2400 AD? When the history of the death penalty is being written, you will have a part in it as you have a part in this book. Writing will keep your memory alive for a long, long time.

I was glad to hear Michael is OK. I saw that his birthday was this month when I was going through old letters, so I sent him birthday wishes by e-mail but I haven't heard from him. I think your advice to him is very good – alerting him to the fact that he's somebody that's needed in this world, he's not alone but is cared for. As you say, it sure must be unpleasant for you to see him so down when 'he's withstood all the judgements and other cruel things in life'. As you say, there's a deeper reason for his ill-health and depression. And then he's so much on his own. Maybe you get more support and understanding from some of your fellow prisoners than he gets outside? I don't know.

* * *

*You shouldn't worry about making slow time with* We're All Doing Time, *it took me a while to read it. I truly didn't buckle down until I was in lock-up and then I had plenty of time on my hands without a TV. I think books like that one are just meant to be read when needed.*

*The e-mail from Benny was interesting. I thought it was crazy they gave Louis and Steve five months in jail for just protesting. That was over outrageous if you ask me. It's certainly obvious that Ladon took his faith seriously to give up all he did to go and live the life he chose. The suggestion made about the Cross implying the intersection of personal choice taken at great personal cost in the face of societal values, I thought that was good food for the body, soul and spirit.*

*It was evident to me that there was lots of very wise people in Benny's company. Veronique sounded like the most interesting of all, at least what he spoke of her was intriguing to me.*

*All of them sounded to be right in their own right. It seems that each person he spoke of was at some point faced with a gut-checking moment, but then, I guess, we all at some point or another as human beings are confronted with those kind of moments, huh? Jim from Canada using the story of Fionn to withstand those long days and nights over in Iraq chained up for over three months, was something.*

*I thought Fionn was truly a noble warrior. The tests he went through were something. I like the motto: 'Truth in our hearts, strength in our limbs and deeds according to our words.' I like that and I like to think my life has somewhat resolved around that and will continue to form around that.*

*Why was Tom Fox taken and executed? Was this in the news? Was it an isolated incident? Why wasn't the others? Who was they held by? A political group? What do you think Benny meant when he said Veronique was talking about 'the struggle between light and dark and how we all experience it in our daily lives, but maybe not as extreme as in the bigger scenario'? What do you think she meant by that? I do agree with what Sybille said about sometimes the right question is much more important than the answer to it. Because it's thought-provoking? Or would you say there's another reason beyond it?*

*There's no more news and opinion to report, so I'll end this now and let you get back to what you was about to do before I interrupted you! I do hope all is well. Say Hi to the rest of the family for me and take care and be safe.*

Last week three Afghan asylum-seekers who were staying in a hostel down the country were arrested by the Guards. It seems somebody (working in the hostel?) reported to the Guards that they had suspicious electrical wires and tools in their room, and the rumours spread like wildfire that the stuff was for bomb making and that they were going to blow themselves up during one of the St Patrick's Day parades, and then the racist calls started coming in to the local radio stations and it was all very ugly. . . . Our friend Rahim knew the men involved and he got on to his solicitor in Dublin to explain that the tools were used for fixing cars and bikes. The solicitor then got on to the Guards and the fellows were released. But I'm not sure if they are going to drop the case or not, and the men are considering taking a case for wrongful arrest. The three of them were sleeping in one room – great accommodation! – the tools belonged to just one fellow but they were all caught up in the case. And what made matters worse was that the Guards searched the whole hostel, annoyed everybody and found small amounts of hash with a few people, and they [the people found with the hash] were also very annoyed!

I was at an anti-war march in Dublin on Saturday, five years after the invasion of Iraq. It was pouring rain but there was a fair crowd, five to six hundred. Some of the reports from Iraq are awful. There was also a live link to Gaza. The protests have fallen away in numbers in a big way – 150,000 marched in 2003. In Ireland it has now got very hard to get a crowd out on the streets, the economy is very slow, lots of people thinking of themselves. Government is fairly gutless, won't admit what the whole country knows, i.e. that the US is flying prisoners on planes through Shannon and on to countries that allow torture. 'We believe Bush' is their answer, more or less. Our prime minister is in Washington today and will give Bush a bowl of shamrock!

The book I went to Conamara to finish – I got the page proofs of it the other day to read and correct – so it shouldn't be long until the book is out! It reads OK, I think, there's a bit of movement in it, even if I say so myself! Humility? I would never have finished it without going to the solitude of Conamara. But it's totally in Irish, Ray! It tells the story of a Traveller girl from the day she's born to her wedding day.

About a hundred yards down the road there is a shop where we get the paper, milk and so on. A man sells *The Big Issue* outside the shop every Friday and Saturday – it's a paper about homelessness, I saw it in Chicago also. The guy who sells it, his name is Nikolai, he's from Romania and he came to Ireland as an asylum-seeker and was allowed stay. I think the police beat him up, one eye is badly damaged and he still has health problems.

Anyway, he stands there all day, 10 AM to 6 PM, so I said why don't you get an MP3 or something like it to listen to music to pass the time. He was horrified! 'I am a Pentecostal Christian. No drink, no smoking, no music.' And then he joined his hands: 'Only music to Jesus in church.' He goes to church three times a week. When I was saying goodbye, I said: 'You are a good Christian.' 'Oh yes,' he said, 'a very good Christian'!

I was going to tell him about 2Pac [Tupac Shakur] but I thought, maybe not. I think I would prefer your attitude to music than his. It takes all kinds. But Nikolai is a nice guy and we have a little chat every week, his English is improving slowly.

Goretti will be back soon. I must e-mail her to get some postcards, I completely forgot you asked me about that.

A Cathal story – he was in Galway lately for a couple of days with his mom and he thought he was in heaven (tractors, trailers, calves, silage, sheep!). He was here one day making kind of spluttering noises with his mouth. Who told you how to do that, Cathal? 'The baby' – followed by a huge laugh. Who told you, Cathal? 'Not the baby! Mammy!' – and another laugh. We think he is the cutest! Catherine and Séamus have colds. Eoin won their last match after a 1–0 defeat the previous week, Róisín is stopping all incoming forwards in their tracks! Francis says the boys are much more serious, the girls have a laugh even during the match! A promise – much less grandchild talk from now on! Promise.

Bríd and myself are fine, no problems. I was at the heart doctor a few weeks ago – my heart still has an irregular beat but the doc says 'You're good'. I didn't ask him was he sure!

I don't think there is any more news, Ray, on this trip to Ireland, and we took no photos lately either. We will be thinking of you, Ray, and hoping you can stay calm and focused. I was moved when Jim told me that you wanted your family to know from this book what you have become. I'm sure they know that already without any work of mine. All best wishes, dear friend.

*I wouldn't like the racist chants that go up at the games, that wouldn't sit well with me at all. I doubt if that would even be accepted over here in the States by the arena, let alone by black fans. That's a good way to incite a riot. That's left a bad taste in my mouth, I doubt if I'll ever be in attendance at one of those matches.*

*I have a question. Would it be possible to have the hubs stolen from in front of the house without it being noticed? I'm thinking it happened in town, it was either a druggie or someone with a Mazda 323.*

*The birthday party for Francis sounded like it was my kind of party. Did you take pictures? I would've enjoyed myself there, I would've stayed probably until 4 AM. I'm in good shape. Yesterday I weighed in at 208lbs, that's good for 6' 1". I've been hitting them weights about four months hard, three times a week. Some ball skills now and then I'll be ready to shine!*

You are perfectly right, Ray, about the racist chants, some of them are very ugly – making monkey sounds is one of the milder ones. In the UK the soccer people have an anti-racist campaign and so on, they ban guilty supporters if they can catch them. The rivalry between some clubs goes overboard altogether, groups of supporters are kept in separate parts of the stadium, and sometimes at a match between Glasgow Rangers and Glasgow Celtic, for example, one lot of supporters are let out first by separate exits and funnelled down the streets by the police so that they don't meet the other lot of supporters. Those two clubs have a long history, Celtic were Catholic/Irish and Rangers were Protestant/English – that has faded now, especially since the two clubs have a lot of foreign players who have most un-Irish or English names! I know a priest who works in Colombia in South America in a very dangerous situation, and when he's home he always goes to Scotland for a Rangers/Celtic match and he thinks the chants are great fun! Strange world!

I think you're totally correct about the hubcaps – the night they were stolen I had parked down a side street and that is the more likely place. Somebody who had a Mazda, as you say. I'm trying a few second-hand places but hubcaps are scarcer than you think! Every time he comes to the house Cathal stops to examine the wheels – he knows there's something different, he misses nothing!

* * *

*You know the second part of the phrase 'Jack of all trades' that you shared, 'master of none', I'd never heard that part of it before, so you enlighten me. Also I'd never heard the saying 'dab hand', thanks for adding it to my vocabulary. That was an interesting quote you sent me from Paul Getty that 'The meek shall inherit the earth but not the mineral rights'!*

*I found it touching what you said about sending wishes and prayers my way when you think of me and want me to be in your company.*

*I remember once you was wondering where did the grandkids learn certain words. Well, now I know from what you was trying to get Cathal to say after he gave his chickenpox a shoooo out the door – you shouldn't be trying to get him to say that he gave the chickenpox a kick in the ass out the door! His mother mightn't be too pleased! All I remember about getting chickenpox is that I could stay home from school.*

*I wouldn't doubt it at all that my letters differ from the first ones we wrote – I trust you more and I'm more comfortable with you, so that always causes one to open up more, as one wouldn't when those things is limited or not there.*

*Yes, I can see the sky from my cell if I look out my tray hole out the window. I'll get you some pictures of my view soon. . . . Yes, there is heat here but no air conditioning. It gets cold here – the prison is not new and the walls have no type of insulation in them, so when it's cool or the temps drop when the sun go down at night, it fills the building with coolness. But I would rather be cold than hot any day.*

*Thank you both for your cards, both put a smile on my face and I enjoyed them. I felt bad for not sending you all a card for Easter and St Patrick's Day, honestly they both kind of snuck up on me. Sorry. And I didn't just not send you all any, I didn't get any out to no one so it really did sneak up on me this year.*

*Nikolai sounds like he's a good guy, a devoted Christian, but I think he needs to take it down some, I've never heard of listening to music being wrong to Christians. About my MP3, it's on its last legs. I've dropped it more times than I want to admit. The last time I dropped it the screen didn't come on again and a couple hundred of the songs disappeared. Honestly, I was afraid or more embarrassed to tell you, so that's why it never came up, but since you asked I can't lie about it. If I promised I'll be more careful, could I get another one for my birthday? . . . You asked me about some books. Do you know the last two didn't never get here to me. No, I'm not really reading so there is no need to order any right now.*

*I understood what you were saying about the Glasgow Rangers/Celtic matches. I understand now from the history you told me why the match trouble could be so serious. Over here that's not allowed, even if it's not a written rule, the fans wouldn't go along with it. There may be some isolated incidents but not a group half the size of the stadium. That's distasteful if you ask me – not that anybody did!*

*So the answers I gave to the questionnaire you sent me show that I would be furthest away from McCain, that's a pleasure to know. I was hoping I'd be closest to Barack but I guess not, huh? I'll still vote for Obama if given the chance.*

In late September 2007, the US Supreme Court imposed a *de facto* moratorium on death-row executions pending its hearing of the case of *Baze* v. *Rees* into the constitutionality or otherwise of the lethal-injection procedure in the state of Kentucky. This was to become a seven-month moratorium, the longest period of time without an execution since a seventeen-month moratorium that stretched from 1981 into late 1982. On 16 April 2008, the Supreme Court ruled in a majority decision that the lethal-injection procedure did not constitute cruel and unusual punishment. Within days, the state of Georgia said that it would recommence executions, and on 7 May it executed William Earl Lynd (53) for the murder of his girlfriend in 1988.

As executions resumed, Levon 'Bo' Jones became the 129th person to be freed from death row since 1976, and the fifth since September 2007, after evidence that he was innocent of the crime for which he had been sentenced emerged. He's the eighth wrongly convicted death-row inmate out of North Carolina alone and the second to be freed after evidence of police misconduct was brought to light.

A statement from the National Coalition to Abolish the Death Penalty said that during the seven-month moratorium 'States that are now gearing up to resume executions did absolutely nothing to assure that society's ultimate sanction is fair or accurate. Levon Jones spent thirteen years on death row, and had he been an inmate in Alabama, Oklahoma, Texas or Virginia, it is quite likely he would be dead today – and the truth buried with him. This is proof positive that we don't need to return to business as usual. States should suspend executions until they have examined their system and can assure us that innocent people are not at risk of execution'.

The NCADP said that the Supreme Court decision sidestepped the critical issues surrounding the death penalty. The organisation's executive director, Diann Rust-Tierney, said: 'The death-penalty system was a flawed public policy before the Supreme Court agreed to review Kentucky's lethal-injection protocol. It was a flawed public policy while the Court debated the protocol. And now that the Court has ruled, it remains as deeply a flawed public policy as ever.'

The relatively narrow scope of the Court's deliberations did not address basic issues of fairness, bias, ineffective counsel or innocent people being convicted and sentenced to death, Rust-Tierney said. She pointed out a number of remarkable events that had occurrred since the last execution, on 24 September 2007: five names have been added to the list of people freed from death row after evidence of their innocence emerged, bringing that number to at least 129; New Jersey has abolished the death penalty; Nebraska has no effective death penalty after its Supreme Court ruled the electric chair unconstitutional; the American Bar Association has called for a nationwide moratorium on executions; and the United Nations, reflecting evolving trends around the globe, has voted for a worldwide moratorium. In addition, Rust-Tierney said, California and Tennessee have held state hearings in order to study their respective death-penalty systems, and constitutional questions relating to the death penalty have been raised in New Hampshire and New Mexico. 'And that's just in seven months. It seems that the more we learn about the death penalty, the more we learn we can live without it,' Rust-Tierney concludes.

Justice Stevens, who sided with the majority in the Supreme Court decision, warned that debate will continue, not just over lethal-injection protocols 'but also about the justification for the death penalty itself'.

*Today we lost one of four games on the b-ball court, I didn't do much running. I washed some clothes and cleaned my cell out, swept and mopped it, it smells fresh, like it got cleaned today!*

*I fear I have lost contact with Michael. His phone is down so I write and send postcards but no reply. You asked about the inmates here and whether they have contacts with free-world people. For the most part I would say yes, because there's so many outside groups that befriend and support us. But some guys just don't write. So yes, there are guys here who don't have outside contacts or people to send them $.*

*And you also asked about flowers and nature – no, we really don't get the chance to see or smell flowers and their fragrance. We see more like the weeds around the gates or fences leading out to the walk yard, and whether there will be colors depends on the season. Mostly purple is out there or yellow, but again they're only weeds. But you find contentment in what you got, you know?*

# Epilogue

*Questions?*

*Life isn't predictable,*
*but if it were, what would we wish for?*
*Days and no nights? Calm and no fright?*
*All ups and no downs?*
*Too much of a good thing can be bad.*
*If it rains, why are you sad?*
*Do you miss the sun?*
*April showers bring May flowers.*
*If you're uncomfortable,*
*Do you feel what you need to do?*
*If you only felt love, what of pain?*
*To be able to wish it away*
*Is that a loss or a gain?*

*I first will say 'thanks to you' for deeming me worthy of your time that you spent reading this collection of thoughts. And I must give thanks to the good Lord Almighty for I know without him none of this would be possible, this blessing of being able to reach out. . . . Being a product of my environment has made my road travelled bumpy, full of potholes, but somehow with the graces I've made it this far and I'm sane.*

*Let it be known that I am very sorry for the pain and hurt I've caused to all. My crime is one that's caused someone's death and for those people that's been affected by this, I'm very apologetic. If I could rewind time I would do so many things differently, starting from the first time I was hurt and disappointed by someone I cared deeply for. Family of my victim, forgive me for hurting you and disrupting your lives. For that I'll never forgive myself, for I've done time on top of every moment, no more or less.*

*My past will drive me crazy and my future will kill me dead!*

*So what will you do, if you was me?*

*Being labeled as a death-row inmate, causing people's family hurt, isn't who I want to be remembered as, so hopefully after you set this book down, you'll have had a better look into the eyes of a manchild. I still haven't forgiven myself, but with this book it almost feels like a start.*

What are my thoughts now that we've got this far, right out to page whatever this is?

As Ray peeps out from his eight-foot-by-five-foot existence, it must seem to him that I have an active, rich and varied life. Sometimes I fear that I may sound too carefree when I'm writing to Ray. Should I tone down the colour of my life, try to make it less interesting, more monochrome than technicolour? Then I remember one of the first bits of advice Michael gave me: 'Tell Ray everything you can about the free world. He wants to keep in touch with that world, the world in which he can no longer play a part. Show him your world; show him the bigger world.'

As the time of publication draws near, the news comes from Ray that Michael's health is improving and that these two long-time friends are in regular contact again. That is great and happy news. There is more very happy news. Hamid has been given refugee status, he can stay in Ireland, he is safe. Rahim continues to struggle in his limbo existence. And yes, of course Rahim and all the other asylum-seekers are very grateful for their weekly allowance of €19.10! An allowance that has remained unchanged since 2000, despite many representations from justice groups and concerned individuals.

It is necessary to refer to the Bible and to Catholic teaching on the death-penalty issue. Nothing I have read leads me, as a Christian, to believe that capital punishment is fair and justified. I believe that it is an ugly and cruel system, and I wonder how those who operate the system can look each other in the eye. It is a system unworthy of any decent or Christian society. Yet it seems that it is Christians who can quote the Bible who are among the foremost defenders and advocates of the system.

Chapter 13 of Paul's Epistle to the Romans states that civil authority is 'the servant of God to execute wrath on the wrongdoer' (Revised Standard Version). There is no mention of that lode word 'execute' in the Jerusalem Bible, which states that authorities 'carry out God's revenge by punishing wrongdoers'. The word 'execute' does not appear in the Greek text and had to be added so that the English text would read properly. The words from Matthew's Gospel 'he who lives by the sword dies by the sword' are also used to defend the use of the death penalty, but Sr Helen Prejean points out that it is clear from the context that Jesus was warning his apostles not to use their swords to defend Him lest violence beget violence.

Another biblical quotation used to defend the death penalty is 'an eye for an eye' (Exodus 21). To the people who use these quotations, God is a God of wrath, not the God of love; they disregard the urging of Christian churches for the past sixty years to look beyond the literal meaning of biblical passages.

In the phrase 'an eye for an eye', a person who has taken the eye of another in a fight is instructed to give his own eye in compensation. However, in the New Testament Sermon on the Mount, Jesus urges his followers to turn the other cheek when confronted by violence: 'You have heard that it was said, "An eye for an eye and a tooth for a tooth". But I say to you, do not resist an evildoer. If anyone strikes you on the right cheek, turn to him the other also.' (Matthew 5, 38–39)

The passage continues with the importance of showing forgiveness to enemies and those who harm you. This exhortation of Jesus can be taken as implying that 'an eye for an eye' encourages excessive vengeance. Some theologians see this difficult message of love as a badge of distinction for Christianity, but the religious texts of other belief systems have similar teachings.

When Catholic church leaders referred to the value and dignity of life, they were usually referring only to the issues of abortion and euthanasia. Pope John Paul II challenged the death penalty more than any other pope, but the 1992 version of the Catholic Catechism stuck to the traditional teaching of Thomas Aquinas regarding the common good and defence of society. According to Aquinas, legitimate public authority had the right and the duty to punish wrongdoers 'by means of penalties commensurate with the gravity of the crime, not excluding, in cases of extreme gravity, the death penalty'. Those last ten words gave joy to advocates of capital punishment.

However, an ever-increasing number of secular and religious institutions all over the world began to voice their grave and increasing concern about the death penalty, and the death penalty was abolished in a number of countries. In January 1997, a Vatican statement said that a change would be made to the Catholic Catechism in view of 'progress in doctrine' about the death penalty, and in September of the same year those all-important last ten words were removed from the Catholic Catechism. Henceforth, Catholics were to accept that no matter how terrible the crime, the death penalty was not to be imposed.

In August 2008, the press office of the Irish Catholic Hierarchy sent me a long statement on the death penalty, pointing out that the Church's Magisterium has spoken out with increasing frequency in defence of the sacredness and inviolability of human life. The statement said that the encyclical letter *Evangelium Vitae* by Pope John Paul II, which was published in March 1995, condemned the use of the death penalty, since the only potentially acceptable use of the death penalty is when it would not otherwise be possible to defend society, a situation that is rare if not non-existent today.

The encyclical again states that punishment ought not go to the extreme of executing the offender except in cases of absolute necessity: in other words, when it would not be possible otherwise to defend society. Today, however, as a result of steady improvements in the organisation of the penal system, such cases are very rare, to the point of being practically non-existent. In any event, the principle set forth in the new Catechism of the Catholic Church remains valid: 'If bloodless means are sufficient to defend human lives against an aggressor and to protect public order and the safety of persons, public authority must limit itself to such means, because they better correspond to the concrete conditions of the common good and are more in conformity to the dignity of the human person.'

Also, in a pastoral letter dedicated to the subject of capital punishment and published in December 2005, the Catholic Bishops' Conference of the United States said: 'In Catholic teaching the State has the recourse to impose the death penalty upon criminals convicted of heinous crimes if this ultimate sanction is the only available means to protect society from a grave threat to human life. However, this right should not be exercised when other ways are available to punish criminals and to protect society that are more respectful to human life.'

How worrying to read the November 2007 report from the Equal Justice Initiative that more than seventy children aged thirteen and fourteen years of age have been condemned to 'death in prison' in the US. According to the EJI, most of the sentences were mandatory, and the age or life history of the children were not considered. Some were charged with crimes that did not involve homicide, many were convicted of crimes for which adults or older teenagers were chiefly responsible, and nearly two-thirds were children of colour.

In the US, more than 2,200 juveniles, aged seventeen or younger, have been sentenced to life imprisonment without parole. All these cases raise serious legal and moral issues; the sentences should be changed to parole-eligible sentences as quickly as possible. The EJI has launched a campaign to challenge the 'death in prison' sentences imposed on children, some of whom have been without legal help for so long that the obstacles to winning relief in court could be great. The EJI says that greater public awareness, along with informed activism, are needed to reform policies and practices that now hold no hope for children and other juveniles.

One of the good things about the prison where Ray is incarcerated is that it allows contact visits. The joy with which he hugs his mother, his family and the couple of friends who visit him must be indescribable. That warm human contact might very well be keeping him sane.

When Ray and myself exchange stories of his daughter, nephew and nieces, and my grandchildren, we are happy and thankful, and yet anxious for their welfare at the same time. Groups of boys fighting each other, finding ways of getting into games and cinemas without paying, smoking on the quiet. Things that boys do all over the world, things that Ray and I did, each in our own way. When I think of these things, I find it hard to believe that Ray is on death row. When he comes into my mind, as he does frequently every day, the whole situation seems unreal. Is the person whom I know to be kind and gentle really there in a cell in a faraway death-penalty US state? Could it happen that he will be executed?

Our letters come and go in an easy rhythm, and when he is coping well – 'maintaining', as he puts it – you could almost persuade yourself that these are just ordinary letters from an ordinary friend. But that image of the eight-foot-by-five-foot cell is never far away. People often ask 'How is Ray?', and I say he is great. That is true. Other times, I say 'Ray is fine', but I'm never certain if that is true or not. Perhaps I will never know unless I visit him.

# Appendix 1: The Current Situation

## States Without the Death Penalty (14)

Alaska, Hawaii, Iowa, Maine, Massachusetts, Minnesota, New Jersey, New York, North Dakota, Rhode Island, Vermont, West Virginia, Wisconsin and Puerto Rico, as well as the District of Columbia *(as of June 2008)*

## States With the Death Penalty (36)

Alabama, Arizona, Arkansas, California, Colorado, Connecticut, Delaware, Florida, Georgia, Idaho, Indiana, Illinois, Kansas, Kentucky, Louisiana, Maryland, Mississippi, Missouri, Montana, Nebraska, Nevada, New Hampshire, New Mexico, North Carolina, Ohio, Oklahoma, Oregon, Pennsylvania, South Carolina, South Dakota, Tennessee, Texas, Utah, Virginia, Washington and Wyoming *(as of June 2008)*

## The Five States with the Most Executions Since 1976

Texas (410), Virginia (101), Oklahoma (87), Missouri (66) and Florida (65)

## The Five States with the Biggest Death Rows

California (669 inmates), Florida (388), Texas (370), Pennsylvania (228) and Alabama (201)

Even the most enthusiastic supporter of the death penalty in the US must realise that there is a practical limit to capital punishment. With about 3,500 prisoners on death row, it would take one execution a day for ten years to clear the backlog.

The central federal government of the USA and the US military have their own death-penalty process. Timothy McVeigh was the first federal death-row prisoner to be executed in the US since the 1963 execution by hanging of Victor Feguer. Jean Raul Garza and Louis Jones were executed, both by lethal injection, in 2001 and 2003, respectively. The federal death penalty can be enacted in any state or territory of the United States, even in states that do not have the death penalty. The US Attorney-General, in consultation with a panel of five lawyers, decides whether the death penalty will be sought. The federal death penalty has been expanded in recent years to include about sixty different offences, including murder committed in the course of drug dealing, murder of certain government officials, kidnapping resulting in death, murder for hire, fatal drive-by shootings, sexual-abuse crimes resulting in death and car-jacking resulting in death.

The US is divided into ninety-four federal districts, and local attorneys must submit all potential death-penalty cases to the attorney-general for review and for a decision as to whether to seek the death penalty. There are racial and geographical disparities in federal death-penalty prosecutions.

According to a Justice Department study published in 2000, in 80 percent of the cases in which a federal prosecutor sought the death penalty in the previous five years, the defendant has been a member of a minority ethnic group; in more than half the cases, the defendant has been an African-American. According to an analysis of 146 federal death-penalty cases since 1988, 60 percent of white defendants avoided a death sentence through plea-bargaining; only 41 percent of black defendants had the same outcome.

Although one might expect federal law to be applied evenly throughout the country, from 1995 to 2000, 42 percent of the federal cases submitted to the attorney-general for review came from just five of the ninety-four federal districts. Including the twenty-one districts that have never submitted a case for review by the attorney-general, forty of the federal districts never recommended seeking the death penalty for any defendant.

US attorneys who have most frequently sought federal death penalties are from states with high numbers of state executions. There are over twenty defendants on federal death row, the majority from just three states: Texas, Virginia and Missouri.

The US military has its own death-penalty statute. In March 2008, the US government decided to seek the death penalty against six Guantánamo Bay detainees who are accused of having played central roles in the attacks of 9/11. The defendants will be tried before Military Commissions, which are not part of either the federal criminal-justice system or the military's justice system for its own members. The laws and procedures under the Military Commission Act of 2006 have not been tested and had to be rewritten after the government's first attempt to try a case in this way was found to be unconstitutional.

Some experts have stated that the trials of the detainees will be a 'historic challenge' for prosecutors. Eric Freedman, a law professor who has consulted with the detainees' lawyers, noted that a decision to seek the death penalty will draw 'intense scrutiny' to the proceedings 'both legally and politically from around the world'. Seeking the death penalty could also bog down the military court system, noted Tom Fleener, a former military defence lawyer, particularly since there are many unanswered legal questions, such as how to handle evidence obtained through coercive methods. He stated: 'Neither the system is ready, nor are the defence attorneys ready to do a death-penalty case in Guantánamo Bay, Cuba.'

If the detainees are convicted and sentenced to death, there is an appeals process, though it is not yet clear whether inmates will have access to the writ of habeas corpus, one of the fundamental ways to challenge a death sentence. There is no execution chamber at the detention camp in Guantánamo Bay, Cuba, where the detainees are being held.

In July 2008, George W. Bush signed a request by the US military that Ronald Gray be executed following his court-martial conviction in 1988 on charges of murder and rape. A member of the US armed forces cannot be executed until the president approves the death sentence. This would be the first execution of a member of the military since 1961. The last president to act on a military death sentence was John F. Kennedy, who commuted a death sentence to life in prison in 1962.

# Appendix 2: The Future

In 2000, a *New York Times* survey found that during the previous twenty years, the murder rate in states with the death penalty has been 50 to 100 percent higher than in states without the death penalty. Ten of the twelve states which were then without the death penalty had murder rates below the national average, whereas half of the states with the death penalty had homicide rates above the national average. In 2006, the FBI crime report pointed out that southern states had the highest murder rate and accounted for over 80 percent of executions; the north-east had less than 1 percent of executions and had the lowest murder rate.

Psychologists believe that the threat of execution at some future date is unlikely to enter the minds of those who are in the grip of fear or rage, those who are panicking while committing another crime such as a robbery, those who suffer from mental illness or mental handicap and do not fully understand the gravity of their crime, or those acting under the influence of drugs or alcohol, or both.

A Harris poll in 2004 showed that only 41 percent of US adults believe that the death penalty deters people from committing murder. This is the smallest number from all the Harris polls carried out since 1977 that asked about the value of the death penalty as a deterrent. Over 80 percent of former and current presidents of the top US academic criminological societies reject the idea of the death penalty as a deterrent.

Public support for the death penalty remains strong in the US, the only western democracy which executes murderers. Since

1936, Gallup has been asking Americans: 'Are you in favour of the death penalty for a person convicted of murder?' The percentage of Americans in favour of the death penalty has varied significantly over the years, from a low of 42 percent in 1966, during a revival of the anti-death penalty movement, to a high of 80 percent in 1994. In recent years, polls have shown that support for the death penalty has been more stable, with about two in three Americans supporting it – 65 percent in 2006, according to a Gallup poll.

Americans support the death penalty even though only a minority think it is a deterrent and almost everyone (95 percent) believes that innocent people are sometimes convicted of murder.

Members of the US public believe that, on average, 11 percent of all those convicted are innocent. African-Americans put the figure much higher. But the two-thirds of the public who support the death penalty seem to feel that that is an acceptable price to pay. There seems to be a certain inconsistency here. Only one third said, when asked, that they would still support the death penalty if they believed that a substantial number of innocent people were convicted of murder, and almost half said that they would oppose it in the same circumstances. But if 11 percent are wrongly convicted, is that not 'substantial'?

Eighty percent of Republicans and 58 percent of Democrats support the death penalty, and 74 percent of men support it, compared to 62 percent of women. There are substantial differences between whites and blacks in their support for capital punishment. The data show that 71 percent of whites support the death penalty, compared with only 44 percent of blacks. Blacks are also, no doubt, aware of the fact that 98 percent of the chief district attorneys in death-penalty states are white. About 70 percent of Protestants and 66 percent of Catholics support the death penalty; support is much lower (57 percent) among those of no particular religious persuasion. Approximately 50 percent of the US public now prefer life without parole as an alternative to the death penalty.

In the last three years the number of death sentences in the US has been lower than at any time since the death penalty was reinstated in 1976. The number of executions has also declined: there were ninety-eight executions in 1999, and fifty-three in 2006. In 2007, there were just forty-two executions: twenty-six in Texas, sixteen in other states. There were no executions in twenty-five states that have the death penalty.

In 1977, just sixteen countries had abolished the death penalty for all crimes. However, Amnesty International claims that, as of January 2008, 135 countries are now abolitionist in law or in practice. 'I think Michigan made a wise decision 150 years ago,' said the state's governor, John Engler, a Republican, in 2000. He was referring to the state's abolition of the death penalty in 1846. 'We're pretty proud of the fact that we don't have the death penalty.'

The National Coalition to Abolish the Death Penalty gives as one of its reasons for stating that capital punishment is a flawed policy the fact that life without parole is a sensible alternative to the death penalty, and also the fact that almost every state in the US now has the capacity to sentence a person to life in prison without parole. A sentence of life without parole generally means exactly what it says: the person is locked away in prison until they die. Unlike the death penalty, a sentence of life in prison without parole allows mistakes to be corrected. The life-without-parole argument seeks to win support for the abolition of the death penalty, and it is hard to disagree with those who put it forward.

There is unrelenting retribution in the 'three strikes and out' policy and in its sister policy of life without parole. Is there no place for forgiveness, ever? To a nineteen-year-old – just over the cut-off point for the death penalty – life without parole must seem extremely cruel and inhumane, continual punishment, with neither forgiveness nor a chance to make a second start. One wonders what Christ would say. Yet life without parole must be tolerated as a bad alternative to death by lethal injection.

Life in prison without parole is a terrifying prospect and probably much more depressing now, if that is possible, than it was twenty years ago. Terry Kupers is a California-based psychiatrist who has toured many of the super-maximum security prisons where an increasing number of death-row prisoners have been placed. Kupers points out that twenty years ago death-row prisoners were not locked down; they were not in isolation. 'So they had a prison life, but it was a life where they could be out on the yard and have some meaningful activities.' Now in an increasing number of states, these inmates spend almost all of their time in their cells. Some lawyers argue that the sentence their clients were given was not solitary confinement nor psychological torture.

There is a real possibility that severe isolation, lock-down and restrictive confinement in 'super-max' prisons, and the lengthy and uncertain interval between sentence and execution, leads to the 'volunteerism' we have mentioned already, whereby prisoners forego all their appeals, believing that life without parole is *not* better than being dead. According to the Death Penalty Information Center in Washington, since 1976 there have been about 130 death row 'voluntary' executions, representing 12 percent of all executions.The US has a higher rate of incarceration than at any other time in its history, state budgets are pressed to breaking point, and public services are being slashed – including education, which should have a central role in crime prevention. There are 2.3 million adults in federal and local jails (or 1 in 99 adults, out of a total adult population of 230 million). Over 11 percent of black men aged twenty to thirty-four is incarcerated, compared to 1.6 percent of white men in the same age group.

The US, with its 'prison-happy' approach, leads the world in in terms of the proportion of the population behind bars. China, with a far greater population, is second, with 1.5 million prisoners, and Russia is third, on 890,000. In the US, Texas tops the league, with 172,000 prisoners. California is the biggest spender on incarceration; thirteen states now spend more than $1 billion each on their prison systems. In 2007, all fifty states between them spent $44 billion on running their prisons, an increase from $10 billion twenty years ago. The above figures are contained in a report from the Washington-based research body the Pew Center on incarceration in the various states. The report concluded that a continual increase in America's reliance on incarceration 'will pay declining dividends in crime prevention. Expanding prisons will accomplish less and cost more than it has in the past'.

Industry and Wall Street investors know that there is a great deal of money to be made from prisons, and they lobby for longer sentences to ensure a ready supply of (low-paid) workers who cannot go on strike. Ten years ago, there were only five private prisons in the US, with 2,000 prisoners. Now there are a hundred private prisons, with 62,000 inmates, and the numbers are expected to increase rapidly.

The prison-industry complex is one of the fastest-growing

industries in the United States, according to a study by the Progressive Labor Party, which notes that 'This multimillion-dollar industry has its own trade exhibitions and websites'. The industry can build its own prisons and supply all the necessary architecture skills, plumbing and food supplies, security guards and 'padded cells in a large variety of colours'. It is estimated that the federal prison industry produces 100 percent of all military helmets, ammunition belts, bulletproof vests, ID tags, shirts, pants, tents, bags and canteens. Along with war supplies, prison workers supply 98 percent of the entire market for equipment assembly services; 93 percent of paints and paintbrushes; 92 percent of stove assembly; 46 percent of body armour . . . the list goes on. Prison labour has its roots in slavery, just as the death penalty is often seen as a hangover from those same bad old days.

Since 1976, there have been more than 129 death-row exonerations. That is probably an unpleasant truth to those Americans who like to think that innocent individuals are not convicted wrongfully and that prosecutors and police investigators abide by the law. But this is far from the truth.

According to Amnesty International, mistaken eyewitness evidence is one of the main factors leading to wrongful convictions, followed by inadequate legal representation, police and prosecutorial misconduct, perjured testimony, racial prejudice, jailhouse 'snitch' testimony, suppression or misinterpretation (or both) of mitigating evidence, and communityor political pressure to solve a case. Sometimes these factors only come to light when DNA testing has proven the innocence of a prisoner.

DNA evidence has brought about a breakthrough in exonerations. DNA identification is based on the universally accepted principle that no two people share exactly the same genetic configuration and that DNA varies from one individual to another. DNA identification is ordinarily admissible to help determine a perpetrator's identity, but in recent years DNA evidence has played a major role in exonerating those who have been wrongly convicted. To date, as many as two hundred innocent 'general population' prisoners have been exonerated by post-conviction DNA testing.

DNA testing must be used where possible, and any reluctance on the part of the criminal-justice system to allow or to admit DNA testing is inexcusable. Prosecutors often oppose it even though DNA evidence can do more than free the innocent, it can also convict the guilty. The state of Virginia executed Joseph O'Dell in July 1997, despite the existence of DNA evidence that could have proved his innocence. The courts refused to consider this new evidence because Virginia law says that any evidence found after twenty-one days is inadmissible in proving the innocence of a convicted person.

The Innocence Project at Benjamin N. Cardozo School of Law, which is run by Barry Sheck and Peter Nuefield, has been giving the lead in bringing DNA testing to the fore. Sheck's aim has been to expand the Innocence Project throughout the nation in order to help inmates obtain and test DNA evidence which can prove their innocence. He has also opened the field for further expansion of DNA testing, as shown by the decision of the first African-American to become a DA in Texas, Craig Watkins, to approve a plan to make available for testing by the Innocence Project DNA gathered in over 350 cases.

Further scientific advances will lead to more exonerations. Already, PCR (Polymerase Chain Reaction), an advance on DNA testing, can deal with minute samples or with old samples of blood and semen. Had these scientific tools been available earlier, many more executions and wrongful convictions could have been avoided.

# SOURCES

Abolish the Death Penalty (*www.deathpenaltyusa.blog-spot.com*)
Amnesty International (*www.amnesty.ie*)
Alt Law Beta (*www.altlaw.org*)
Berkeley Law Death Penalty Clinic (*www.law.berkeley.edu/clinics/dpclinic/*)
Canadian Coalition against the Death Penalty (*www.ccadp.org*)
Citizens United for Alternatives to the Death Penalty (*www.cuadp.org*)
Death Penalty Information Center (*www.deathpenalty-info.org*)
Death Row Speaks (*www.deathrowspeaks.info*)
Democracy Now (*www.democracynow.org*)
Equal Justice Initiative (*www.eji.org*)
Fight the Death Penalty in USA (*www.fdp.dk*)
Front Line (*www.frontlinedefenders.org*)
Human Rights Watch (*www.hrw.org/english*)
Info Wars (*www.infowars.com*)
Innocence Project (*www.innocenceproject.org*)
Insideout (*www.insideout.org/documentaries/dna/thestories3.asp*)
The Justice Project (*www.thejusticeproject.org*)
Law Professors Blogs Network (*www.lawprofessors.type-pad.com*)
Maryland Citizens Against State Executions (*www.md-case.org*)
Moratorium Now (*www.ejusa.org*)
NAACP Defense and Educational Fund (*www.naacpldf.org*)
National Coalition to Abolish the Death Penalty (*www.ncadp.org*)
The New Abolitionist (*www.nodeathpenalty.org*)
*Prison Life* (*www.prisonlife.com*)
Reprieve (*www.reprieve.org.uk*)
Survive Inc (*www.halos.org*)
Thomas Arthur Fight for Life (*www.thomasarthurfightfor-life.com*)

*Dead Man Walking*, Sister Helen Prejean (Fount/Harper Collins)
*Live from Death Row*, Mumia Abu-Jamal (Avon Books, New York)
*Living Justice: Love, Freedom and the Making of The Exonerated*, Jessica Blank & Erik Jensen (Atria Books)
*Manchild in the Promised Land*, Claude Brown (Penguin)
*On a Move: The Story of Mumia Abu-Jamal*, Terry Bisson (Litmus Books)
*Stolen Time*, Sunny Jacobs (Doubleday)
*The Death of Innocents*, Sr. Helen Prejean (Canterbury Press)
*The Exonerated*, Jessica Blank and Erik Jensen (Faber & Faber)
*The Innocent Man: Murder and Injustice in a Small Town*, John Grisham (Random House)
*The Road to Abolition*, Senator Raymond J. Lesniak (The Road to Justice and Peace)

Comunita di Sant'Egidio (*www.santegidio.org*)
Lifelines Ireland, an organisation that defends people on death row in the US and the Caribbean, can be contacted at *paulinegavin@yahoo.co.uk*